HO CHI MINH
LEGEND OF HANOI

HO CHI MINH
LEGEND OF HANOI

Jules Archer

Crowell-Collier Press, New York
Collier-Macmillan Limited, London

JB
Ho-Chi, Minh

Library of Congress Catalog Card Number: 79-151161

The Macmillan Company
866 Third Avenue
New York, New York 10022
Collier-Macmillan Canada Ltd., Toronto, Ontario

Printed in the United States of America

10 9 8 7 6 5 4 3 2 1

Seventh century Vietnamese design element used as chapter opening
illustration drawn by Marjorie Zaum K.

To
Elizabeth A. Jeffreys
and
Dr. W. D. L. Ride
of Perth, Western Australia
in appreciation

Contents

Young Wanderer

HE WAS BORN on May 19, 1890, in a long straw peasant hut in the village of Kim Lien, located in Nghé An, a province of Annam noted for its revolutionaries. "A man born in Nghé An province," cautioned the local proverb, "will oppose anything." The colonial French, who had taken over Indo-China seven years earlier, trusted no native of Nghé An.

Ho was originally named Nguyen Van Thanh ("Nguyen Who Will Be Victorious"), a reflection of his father's revolutionary hopes for his children. Ho's father, Nguyen Sinh Huy, was a minor mandarin (official), who had been a secretary at the Imperial Palace in Hué until his dismissal for showing open hostility toward the new French colonial authority.

He had retreated to rural Kim Lien to support his family by practicing oriental herb medicine and working as a scribe. It was a humiliating loss of face for a Confucian scholar, but allowed him to work closely with a revolutionary movement aimed at pushing the French out of Indo-China.

He involved his whole family. When Ho was ten, his mother died in jail after stealing weapons from French barracks for the independence movement. Ho's older sister Thanh was jailed for similar thefts by a mandarin who said angrily, "Other women bring forth children, while you bring forth rifles!" Before they were nine, Ho and his brother Khiem ran errands and carried messages for the revolutionists.

French colonial administrators, who barred Vietnamese from their parks and clubs, used forced native labor to build their roads. Escaping workers found concealment in the hut of Ho's father, and Ho looked after their needs until it was safe for them to steal away home. Once, to his horror, he saw a laborer recaptured and beheaded on the spot.

At fifteen, wearing his hair tied in two small knots, Ho was sent to a French high school in Hué that accepted Vietnamese children. Learning about the French Revolution and its motto of "Liberty, equality, fraternity," Ho was baffled. How could a people with that revolutionary heritage now themselves oppress the people of Indo-China?

The French had established their colonial rule in Southeast Asia in 1883. They had carved Indo-China into five powerless parts—Cambodia, Laos and three Vietnamese provinces. In southern Vietnam lay Cochin-China with its capital at Saigon. In the north was Tonkin, whose capital was Hanoi. Between them lay Annam, Ho's province, with its capital at Hué.

The French colonial ruling class had sought to re-create an Asiatic France in Indo-China by means of native labor,

at a cost of hunger, disease and squalor. They gave themselves the right to slap awkward Vietnamese waiters who
spilled soup, or rickshaw coolies who dared argue about the
fare.

The colonial government, it was true, had built some
native schools, libraries and hospitals. But it made five
times that expenditure in annual profits from its opium
monopoly alone. The Vietnamese saw the French as an
oppressive clique of feudal barons, tax collectors, customs
men, recruiting sergeants and gendarmes who ignored
Vietnamese culture, law and institutions. Natives who protested or resisted were swiftly and severely punished.

Ho's persistent questions in high school about the significance of the French Revolution brought only evasive re-
plies. His teachers preferred to emphasize the schools,
roads, hospitals and telephone communications the French
had brought to Southeast Asia. But Ho told fellow Vietnamese students, "The first concern of French colonizers is to
make arrangements for their relatives. The next is to grab
and steal as much and as quickly as possible." He managed to get banned books and papers to read, and passed
them to classmates. They learned the story of the stubborn
fight the Vietnamese people had waged against foreign invaders for over two thousand years.

In 40 A.D. the Trung sisters had driven imperial China
from Vietnam, and had ruled as native queens until Chinese arms had reconquered the country. Then the Trung
sisters had committed suicide.

In 1288 A.D. a three-hundred-thousand-man army of the
Mongol Khan had overrun the land, but had been driven
off three times by patriot leader Than Hung Dao. The Ming

dynasty had sought to re-establish Chinese power in 1407 A.D. After a ten-year struggle their forces, too, had been routed by Le Loi.

"Our people," Le Loi declared, "long ago established Vietnam as an independent nation with its own customs and traditions, and these are different from those of the foreign country to the north. We have sometimes been weak and sometimes powerful, but at no time have we suffered from a lack of heroes."

Instead of enslaving or annihilating the defeated Chinese armies, Le Loi charitably provided horses and food for their return home. From then on, accelerating the departure of invading armies became a Vietnamese tradition.

The Chinese subsequently compelled the thirty million Vietnamese to pay tribute to Peking every third year for the right to be let alone, but Vietnam enjoyed a long period of self-rule under Emperor Dai Viet.

The largely Buddhist culture of the Vietnamese had come under the influence of French Jesuit missionaries who arrived in the sixteenth century behind French troops. No more than 10 percent of the population had ever become Catholic, but four centuries after their arrival Ho was complaining, "Catholic missionaries own a fifth of our whole country."

In the 1840's Louis Napoleon sent a fleet to Vietnam on the pretext of punishing the mistreatment of a French missionary. His troops seized Saigon and laid siege to Hué. Annam's army, under King Tu-Duc, avoided frontal battles and took to the jungle. Their guerrilla skirmishes wore down the French, who were also harassed by the steamy rainy season, cholera, scurvy and typhus.

"Everything here," French Admiral Genouilly lamented, "tends toward ruin—men and things."

But by 1884 the French had forced Tu-Duc to surrender, and made themselves the colonial masters of all Vietnam. A revolutionary faction called the Scholars' party had arisen in Annam. Tu-Duc and other Vietnamese monarchs who had yielded to the French were murdered, but the revolt had been crushed during the 1890's. Many of the rebels had fled abroad.

One day in 1910 Ho was caught distributing copies of a banned revolutionary paper. Already suspect as the source of forbidden books on Vietnamese history, he was expelled for "poor grades." His father was privately warned that Ho was headed for a jail cell if he persisted in agitating.

Going south to Cochin-China, Ho found a job at starvation wages teaching school in the little fishing port town of Phan-Thiet, a hotbed of anti-French sentiment.

Here, in 1911, he heard news that thrilled him. The powerful Manchu dynasty of China had been overthrown by a revolution organized from abroad by Sun Yat-sen, who had now returned to head a new Republic of China. With Sun was an Annamese patriot, Pham Boi Chau, who was organizing a Vietnamese Nationalist party in Canton.

Pondering Sun Yat-sen's example, Ho became convinced that only by winning sympathetic support abroad could a revolutionary movement to free Indo-China from the French succeed. Quitting his teaching job, he left for Saigon to attend a trade school that taught cooking and baking. Such skills, Ho knew, would make it easier for him to find work wherever his travels took him.

He decided against joining Pham Boi Chau's group in

Canton, reasoning that the new Chinese republic would be far too feeble to offer much practical help. Some rebel exiles had gone to Japan; but in Ho's eyes, expecting aid from Japan's militarists was to "hunt the tiger and be eaten by wolves."

Who would be more likely to sympathize with the ideals of independence, freedom and democracy, he reflected, than the nations of the West? They, after all, had governments based on the sovereignty of the people. So it was in the West, rather than the East, that he decided to seek help.

In the summer of 1912, barely twenty-two, he secured a job as galley hand aboard the French merchant ship *Latouche-Tréville*. He may have been hastened in this decision by a warrant for his arrest by French security police. The ship carried vacationing colonials between Saigon and Marseilles. Ho wryly noted the sharp contrast between their luxurious food and quarters and the miserable conditions of the crew.

He remained at sea for two years, preparing himself for his mission in the West. All that he saw in his travels around the world deepened his grief and resentment at the suffering of the poor and oppressed of every land.

The *Latouche-Tréville* gave him a far more comprehensive education than any he might have obtained within the walls of a university. Promoted to cook's helper, Ho had ample time at sea to read Shakespeare, Tolstoy, Marx and other great shakers of the world. Visiting Africa, Europe, Australia, South and North America, he worked hard to develop a command of languages that would improve his effectiveness as an international revolutionary. He ended his travels with the extraordinary self-taught ability to speak presentable French, English, Russian, German, Czech and Japanese, as well as three Chinese and several Annamese dialects.

In 1914 he felt ready for Europe. Attracted by the free political climate in England, he left the ship to apply for a kitchen job in London's opulent Carlton Hotel. The kitchen was presided over by the famous French chef Escoffier, who took a personal liking to the slim, quiet Asian youth.

Ho worked first as a dishwasher, then as an apprentice pastry-cook. To send more money home to his father in Kim Lien for the support of his brother and sister, Ho also worked shoveling snow and stoking furnaces in the pre-dawn hours, before reporting at 6:30 A.M. to the Carlton's kitchen.

Although Ho liked London, here, too, he felt dispirited over the vast gulf he observed between the lives of the Carlton's wealthy guests and the army of servants who eked out a bare existence providing them with luxuries. More and more he felt disturbed by the contradictions in Western political practice. Its preachment of liberty and equality for all was inspiring. But why, then, did the West practice social inequality and economic enslavement of the poor?

He helped organize an Overseas Workers' Association to improve working conditions for Asian workers in London, who were barred from British trade unions. When World War I broke out in 1914 he signed up as a seaman for the dangerous Atlantic runs between London, Boston, and New York.

After several trips, one of them made under attack by German U-boats, Ho left the ship in New York. He was driven by curiosity about the United States, and wanted to study at first hand the people who had won their freedom by mounting a revolution against English colonialism.

Working as a waiter in Harlem and Boston, he was shocked by the treatment of American blacks. His views of the United States were ambivalent, influencing his attitude toward the American people for the rest of his life.

"Ah, New York, a great city," he later told an American correspondent. "I spent some time there years ago. I learned a great deal about your country and your people. I have always been impressed with your country's treatment of the Philippines. You kicked the Spanish out and let the Filipinos develop their own country. You were not looking for real estate, and I admire you for that."

But subsequently, while in Moscow, he wrote a blistering attack on American racism as he had observed it. Ho had been appalled, according to Pham Van Dong, by "the barbarities and ugliness of American capitalism, the Ku Klux Klan mobs, the lynchings." Working in the North, Ho could only have observed Klan lynchings in the American press.

Late in 1917 he read that a rebellion had broken out in Vietnam, aided by a mutiny in the French colonial army. He decided to go to France immediately, even though the war was still raging on the battlefields of Normandy. Ho hoped that an overthrow of colonialism in his country was at hand, and determined to do all that he could in Paris to further French support for Vietnamese independence.

The continental French, he believed, were a far more civilized people than the French colonials. In a French port, Marseilles, Ho was addressed as *Monsieur* for the first time in his life—a courtesy never shown to any Vietnamese in his own land.

He arrived in Paris on December 3, 1917, the day that the Russian Bolsheviks opened negotiations with the Germans to get out of the war through a separate peace treaty at Brest-Litovsk. In Ho's view, the Russian people had decided to stop being pawns in an imperialist struggle to divide up the world among colonial powers, and to turn instead to building a socialist Russia.

Establishing contact with other anti-colonial Asians who had come to Paris for jobs as cheap wartime labor, Ho became friends with two Annamese revolutionaries, Phan Van Truong and Phan Chu Trinh. Like him, they saw socialism as the answer for Southeast Asia. Joining them in shabby rooms on the Left Bank, he sought work as a cook.

There were already too many Asian cooks in Paris, so Ho found work as a gardener, laundryman and photo retoucher. Learning enough as a photographer's apprentice to open his own little shop, he advertised, "If you would like a lifelike remembrance of your family, have your photographs retouched at Nguyen Ai-Quôc's." Like all revolutionaries of the day, he went under a number of different names.

Not too successful in his enterprise, he sought to augment his earnings by selling Paris art connoisseurs his own paintings represented as "Chinese antiquities."

His leisure hours were spent attending Sorbonne lectures in French literature, philosophy and Socialist theory. He also sought out in Paris Socialist refugees from other countries to discuss tactics for overthrowing colonialism.

At the end of the war the arrival of President Woodrow Wilson to attend the Versailles Peace Conference gave Ho an idea. Self-determination for all peoples, Wilson had told the world, was the ideal for which the Allies had been fighting. Then why not bring the plight of the Vietnamese under French colonialism to his attention, and persuade him to compel Premier Georges Clemenceau to free Indo-China?

Ho presented his plan to Vietnamese troops who had fought in Normandy with the French army, and were now awaiting transportation home. Applauding, they raised money to send him to Versailles to see Wilson. From a second-hand store Ho rented the first derby and evening suit he had ever worn in his life. Hoping that he now looked important enough to win an audience with the American president, he carefully rehearsed what he would say as the train took him to Versailles.

He knew that Wilson would probably say that immediate independence for Vietnam was not practical. Then he would ask instead for Vietnamese representation in the French parliament, freedom of the press, freedom of assembly, amnesty for political prisoners, government by law instead of decree, and full legal equality of French and Vietnamese.

But in Versailles Ho discovered that he was not alone among nationalists seeking Wilson's ear for a redress of grievances. From all corners of the world representatives of oppressed minorities had gathered to press their claims upon the harassed American president.

"The hungry expect us to feed them, the homeless look to us for shelter, the sick of heart and body depend upon us for cure," Wilson sighed in despair. "What I seem to see—

with all my heart I hope that I am wrong—is a tragedy of disappointment!"

Ho did not get an opportunity to plead the case for Vietnam, despite his persistent efforts to win an interview. He was shocked at the big powers' indifference to the injustices suffered by little countries, especially after all the noble rhetoric that had been used by the Allies during the war to justify their cause. His faith in Wilson died, and with it any illusions of help from the capitalist West.

The cynical settlement at Versailles deepened his conviction that the Socialists were right in charging that the big powers intended to divide up the world as spoils of war, without regard to international justice.

Ho joined the French Socialist party, getting to know Leon Blum and other leading Socialists who, decades later, would head a French government. He made street-corner speeches and wrote articles for the Socialist daily, *Le Populaire*, at the invitation of Karl Marx's grandson, Jean Longuet.

On Christmas Day, 1920, Ho won the right to address the Eighteenth National Congress of the Party as "Comrade Indochinese Delegate." His deep-set black eyes bright with emotion, the thirty-year-old Ho urged his fellow Socialists to aid the Vietnamese struggle against French colonialism.

"In its selfish interest it conquered our country with bayonets," he cried. "Since then we have not only been oppressed and exploited shamelessly, but also tortured. . . . Prisons outnumber schools. . . . Natives having social ideas are arrested and sometimes murdered without trial. . . . Thousands of Vietnamese have been led to a slow death or massacred to protect other people's interests. . . . Comrades, save us!"

But the French Socialist party belonged to the Second International, an association of world Socialist parties that placed national interests first. Ho's appeal was ignored, except for a token expression of sympathy. Bitterly disappointed, he joined a radical faction led by Marcel Cachin to bring the French Socialists into Lenin's Third International, pledged to work for world revolution. Their effort failed.

"If you do not condemn colonialism, if you do not side with the colonial people," Ho reproached the French Socialists, "then what kind of revolution are you waging?"

He studied Lenin's writings on "The National and Colonial Questions," but found them highly complicated. Determined to understand, he read them over and over again until he finally grasped their meaning. He was so excited when he did, he recalled later, that even though he was reading alone in his room in the middle of the night, he cried out to his invisible countrymen, "Dear martyrs, compatriots! This is what we need—this is the path to our liberation!"

He joined Cachin in a bolt from the Socialists to form the French Communist party. Although Ho admired Lenin and the Soviet Revolution, he had little interest in Russian Communism. The Third International appealed to him solely as a world ally in his struggle to free his country from the French.

His new allegiance brought him new friends, including Boris Souvarine, the brilliant Marxist theoretician, and Chou En-lai, a Chinese Communist youth leader who would

one day become second in power in Red China. He joined
them in hot political debates at the Club du Faubourg, a
radical hangout, where he also enjoyed participating in
arguments about hypnotism, astronomy, dreams, death, and
the human soul.

His fellow radicals found the slim, hollow-cheeked, chain-
smoking Oriental a pleasant, mild little man, always charm-
ing and sympathetic, even in the heat of debate. A friend
said of Ho that, with his dry wit, he "seemed always to be
mocking the world and at the same time mocking himself."

The debates at the Club du Faubourg helped him develop fluency in both French and public speaking. Writing
articles for the French Communist paper, *L'Humanité*,
sharpened the cutting edge of his attacks on French indifference to the plight of his people. Verbally and in print
he slashed out at the white racism of French workers, the
French colonial government in Indo-China, the Vietnamese
kings who collaborated. He wrote an anti-French comedy
called *The Bamboo Dragon*, which was performed in the
cabarets of Montmartre.

Yet he was not unmindful of or ungrateful for the political freedom of criticism granted by his hosts. When
Emperor Khai Dinh of Annam arrived in Marseilles for a
visit, Ho wrote him a sarcastic, oddly pro-French, open letter:

"Apart from the racehorses at Longchamp and the pretty
Frenchwomen at the *Opéra*, what else has Your Majesty
deigned to see in the course of your educational visit to this
poetic land of France? The French people are enamored of
justice, freedom and work. Has Your Majesty deigned to
realize this?

"Has Your Majesty received any inkling of the spirit of brotherhood and the deep, noble love of people which animate the people of France, a people who have won their freedom through revolution? . . . Has your august attention ever once been drawn to the existence and achievements of Pasteur, Voltaire, Victor Hugo and Anatole France?"

Through all of his life Ho would never be able to make up his mind whether he hated the French more than he admired them. And the French often felt the same way about Ho.

Roving Revolutionist

IN 1921, with Messali Hadj, an Algerian Communist, Ho started a small anti-colonial monthly called *Le Paria* (The Outcast), urging resistance to French colonialism in Indo-China, Algeria and Morocco. The French minister of colonial affairs, Albert Sarraut, put spies on Ho's trail to report his activities. Amused, Ho offered to save the French their expense by publishing his daily schedule:

"Morning: from 8 to 12 at the workshop. Afternoon: in newspaper offices (leftist, of course) or at the library. Evening: at home or attending educational talks. Sundays and holidays: visiting museums or other places of interest. There you are!"

He became recognized as the spokesman for sixty thousand Indo-Chinese living in France, many of them World War I veterans who had preferred not to return home to colonial rule. They wrote letters about him to their families. Ho's countrymen were fascinated by tales of the shy little expatriate who laughed in the face of French officialdom, and who reproached the French openly for their crimes in Indo-China.

When Ho's friend Nguyen The Truyen returned to Annam for a visit, he was besieged by questions about Ho. Was he just a legend? Did such a man really exist?

In 1922 Ho paid a brief visit to Moscow, the center of the Communist world to which he had given his allegiance. As a French delegate to the fourth World Congress of the Communist International, he met giants of the new Red society—Lenin, Trotsky, and Bukharin. The pleasant little Asian whose gentle manners belied his will of steel made so favorable an impression that he was selected for leadership training at the International School of Marxism in Moscow.

Ho left Paris in 1923 with genuine regret. In the five years he had spent there, he had grown to love the sophisticated city and the many international friends he had made. But his unique charm soon made him equally popular in Comintern (Communist International) circles in Moscow. Attending the University of the Toilers of the East, he also became a member of the Peasant International.

Ho found himself distressed by the European Communist view that world capitalism could only be defeated by an uprising of workers in cities of the West. Hadn't Marx proved wrong in expecting the first Socialist revolution to take place in one of the highly industrialized countries of Western Europe, when it had exploded instead in backward, agrarian Russia? If Ho's own oppressed countrymen had to wait for their freedom until workers in the West first won theirs, the Vietnamese people might well wait forever!

In 1924, at the Fifth Comintern Congress, he delivered a fiery appeal for a change in Comintern policy.

"You will forgive my frankness," he said, "but I cannot avoid explaining that the speeches of my comrades from the mother countries have given me the impression that they are trying to kill a snake by stepping on its tail. For you all know that the venom and the energy of the capitalist snake is concentrated more in the colonies than in the mother countries." The way to topple world capitalism, Ho urged, was not by labor agitation in the West, but by bleeding the capitalists to death in their far-flung colonies.

He pointed out that peasants could wage guerrilla warfare on a shoestring, hiding and fighting in terrain they knew well, while steadily draining the manpower and treasure of the big powers compelled to fight such wars. But first the Comintern had to educate and organize colonial peoples.

"The Annamese people—peasants—live buried in the profoundest night," he explained, "with no newspapers, no conception of what's happening in the world. It's darkness!"

Ho's views won the support of Georgi Dmitrov, the famous Bulgarian revolutionary who headed the Comintern. He named the thin little Asian in a knitted woolen jacket as organizer of the Comintern's Southeast Asia Bureau.

Ho's arguments dovetailed with those of Leon Trotsky, who insisted that a Socialist Russia would not be allowed to survive in a capitalist world, and therefore must mount a world revolution. Joseph Stalin disagreed, insisting that Communist energies be devoted to protecting and developing the Soviet Union first. He wanted the Comintern used principally to harass the capitalist nations by subversion directed at preventing their attack on the USSR.

In 1924, as Lenin lay dying, Stalin and Trotsky were engaged in a power struggle to determine which would suc-

ceed him. Ho carefully avoided taking sides in their ideological clash. Ruth Fischer, a prominent German Communist
working in the Comintern, recalled:

"He immediately won the respect and even the affection
of us all. Amid these seasoned revolutionaries and rigid
intellectuals, he struck a delightful note of goodness and
simplicity. He seemed to stand for mere common decency
—though he was cleverer than he let on—and it was his
well-earned good name which saved him from getting
caught up in internal conflicts. Also, he was temperamen-
tally far more inclined strongly toward action. . . . He
played a very big part in things, bigger than some of the
better-known Asian leaders of the time—Mao did not come
to the fore till later."

Ho's articles began appearing in *Le Paria* under the
pseudonym Nguyen-O-Phap ("Nguyen Who Hates the
French"). When the French Communist party protested
this pen name, he obligingly changed it to Nguyen Ai-Quôc
("Nguyen the Patriot"), by which alias world police were
soon to know him.

"Colonialism is a leech with two suckers," he wrote, "one
of which sucks the metropolitan proletariat and the other
that of the colonies. If we want to kill this monster, we must
cut off both suckers at the same time."

His inflammatory articles reached Annam, worrying the
colonial French, who raided villages in search of Red
cells.

"It's interesting how the French authorities taught our
peasants the words 'Bolshevik' and 'Lenin,'" Ho said later
in amusement. "They began hunting down Communists
among the Annamese peasantry at a time when there wasn't

a trace of a Communist. And that way they spread the propaganda!"

When Sun Yat-sen died in 1925, Moscow-trained Chiang Kai-shek became commander-in-chief of the Chinese Nationalist army. Mao Tse-tung was only a province leader; Chou En-lai and Lin Piao were mere students. Chiang set out to unify China by forcing the warlords in the north to bow to his authority. Stalin sent Soviet military strategist Mikhail Borodin as his envoy to Chiang. Ho was sent along as Borodin's political adviser and interpreter.

But Ho also had won permission for a secret assignment —creating the first Communist organization in Indo-China. He planned to organize it in Canton, southern China, which had become a nationalist center for young Annamese rebels.

Most of these youths were already members of the Vietnamese Nationalist party led by Pham Boi Chau, but were impatient with his lack of militancy. In 1924, when the governor-general of Indo-China visited Canton, some Annamese rebels had hurled a bomb at his car. Chau, blamed, was forced into hiding.

Under the alias Nguyen Ai-Quôc, Ho sought to replace Chau's organization with his own, the Thanh Nien (Association of Revolutionary Annamite Youth). Political rivals later accused him of an act of treachery that, if true, revealed a cynical, ruthless side to the gentle, mild character that charmed all who knew him.

According to this account, Ho had learned of Chau's hiding place and had betrayed it, collecting a reward from the French upon Chau's arrest and extradition to Hanoi for execution. Ho had allegedly said in defense of his act that it hastened rebellion in Vietnam by removing an ineffective leader, inflaming the Vietnamese masses over Chau's execution, and providing funds for a genuine revolutionary movement, his Thanh Nien.

Ho's defenders denied his guilt, pointing out a discrepancy in the story: Chau had not been executed but put under house arrest, and had died naturally 16 years later. There was also the statement by Louis Arnoux, head of the French colonial *Sûreté*, scoffing at a later rumor that Ho had agreed to become a British agent: "Why, I didn't dare ask him to work for *me*—not even at the start of his career!"

Those who knew Ho best did not doubt that he was capable of coolly sacrificing many lives, including his own, to advance his lifelong dream of freedom and independence for his people. Even his Communism was merely a means toward one unchanging end—the destruction of the colonial system in his homeland. Along with guerrilla tactics, the Russians had taught him that revolution could not be waged sentimentally, with qualms; the ends justified the means.

Like many other controversial episodes of his elusive life during the twenties and thirties, the truth about Ho and Chau remained in doubt. Ho himself persistently refused to clarify many of the legends that had grown up about him.

"Ah, but you know, I'm an old man, a very old man," he liked to say with a twinkle in his eye. "And an old man likes to hold on to his little mysteries."

After Chau's arrest, the young Annamese rebels in Canton flocked into Ho's Thanh Nien, and the first Indo-Chinese Communist party was born. The most daring of Ho's disciples were allowed to attend the classes in guerrilla tactics he taught to Chiang Kai-shek's officers at Canton's Russian-built Whampoa Military Academy.

Ho grew especially fond of one of them, Pham Van Dong, son of a mandarin at the court of Hué. Dong had organized a strike in Annam and had been forced to flee to China with the French *Sûreté* at his heels. Ho admired Dong's diligence and cautious pragmatism, and began calling him "my other self" and "my best nephew." Their attachment endured until Ho's death forty-four years later.

The young Annamese in the Thanh Nien were trained for suicide missions in Vietnam. They infiltrated back to organize strikes in schools, plantations, and mines. Ho did not really expect such strikes to succeed, but rather to provoke acts of repression by the French authorities, developing a revolutionary climate. Similar tactics, Ho knew, had worked for Samuel Adams in creating the American Revolution.

Not all the youths who went through Thanh Nien training accepted Marxist doctrine or Communist discipline. Ho regarded the dissidents as unreliable, dangerous to his underground network in Vietnam. Even before they left Canton, their names were leaked by double agents working for the French *Sûreté*. Thus the weakest links of Ho's guerrilla forces were immobilized in French colonial jails, leaving only hard-core Communists to build the revolution.

Communism was being forged in China, too, by Mao Tsetung's army. The Chinese Reds were seizing rich landlords' property and dividing it up among peasants, as well as encouraging factory workers to revolt. Powerful Chinese and foreign business interests, alarmed, offered Chiang Kai-shek full financial support for his Kuomintang (Nationalist People's Party) if he agreed to turn against the Communists.

In 1927, without warning, Chiang attacked the Red Chinese stronghold in Shanghai, slaughtering thousands of workers. A massacre in Nanking and Canton put domestic and foreign Communists to flight. Both the Thanh Nien and Ho's school of guerrilla warfare were swept away in the turmoil.

Forced to flee China, Ho left behind in the region of Hanoi an underground network of 250 Annamite Communists under the direction of Pham Van Dong. They continued organizing strikes in Annam's mines and rubber plantations, but the movement was crippled when Dong was arrested in 1929.

Ho, head shaven and wearing the saffron robes of a Buddhist monk, escaped to Bangkok, Thailand. He slipped through that country, Malaya, Siam, and the Dutch East Indies, setting up small "agitprop" (agitation and propaganda) groups to fight colonialism, some even in Buddhist monasteries.

Although the French *Sûreté* tried hard to get their hands on him, the elusive Ho was like the legendary Scarlet Pimpernel—"they searched for him here, they searched for him there, they searched for him everywhere." Ho would no sooner surface mysteriously in one country than he would swiftly vanish and turn up in another.

In the spring of 1928 he appeared in Moscow, then showed up in Brussels for an anti-imperialist conference attended by Madame Sun Yat-sen, Nehru, and other Asian leaders. He made a brief nostalgic visit back to Paris. Standing on a bridge over the Seine with an old comrade, he murmured, "What a wonderful city, what a wonderful scene!" His friend asked if he didn't think that Moscow, too, was beautiful. "Moscow is heroic," Ho replied, "but Paris is the joy of living!"

After carrying out some Comintern assignments in Italy, Germany and Switzerland, he was ordered to board ship for Hong Kong to attend a secret Thanh Nien congress being held there. The Thanh Nien had fallen into factional disputes after the arrest of Dong. Now only Ho could unify and revive the revolutionary movement in Indo-China.

Slipping unobtrusively into the British crown colony, Ho met "secretly" with Thanh Nien leaders in the bleachers of the Hong Kong Stadium during a soccer match on February 3, 1930. The roar of the crowd drowned out the angry disputes of the feuding leaders, who were assumed by spectators to be arguing over the game below.

Ho, as calm, gentle and persuasive as ever, made peace between the rival factions. He dissolved the Thanh Nien and reorganized it as the frankly labeled Indo-China Communist party.

On February 18 he issued a manifesto announcing the new party and describing its aims: to overthrow French colonialism; to make Indo-China completely independent; to establish a government of workers, peasants and soldiers; to nationalize the banks and confiscate the plantations for division among the peasantry; to end unjust taxes; to establish an eight-hour working day; to restore freedom of speech, press and assembly; to provide universal education; to establish equality of the sexes.

Significantly, free elections were not one of the party's goals. In Ho's eyes, a benevolent dictatorship of the peasantry under Communist direction was sufficient to guarantee just government for Indo-China. He regarded elections as a purely Western idea. There had never been any before the French came, and the French had certainly not been elected. Then why hold elections after they were driven out?

Ho's disciples slipped back into Vietnam to begin a new underground campaign of subversion coordinated by Ho from Hong Kong. Tipped off that he was back in Southeast Asia, Inspector Louis Arnoux sent word to Hong Kong that Ho could count on a large reward if he was willing to turn over the names of ICP (Indo-China Communist party) members operating in Vietnam.

But in a report to the colonial government Arnoux was forced to admit, "It is useless to try to buy him. He is completely disinterested."

Thousands of discontented peasants began flocking into the ranks of the new ICP. Even after French colonialism had been entrenched for half a century, over 80 percent of the Vietnamese still could not read or write. There was only one Western doctor for every fifty thousand Vietnamese. Corrupt landlords and officials kept peasants on the brink of starvation.

On September 12, 1930, the influence of the ICP was evident in a hunger march on Vinh by over six thousand peasants in northern Annam. They seized large estates, divided them up and set up people's soviets. The French colonial government was badly frightened at this demonstration by Ho's cadres of their ability to revolutionize the discontent of the peasantry.

Despite the danger of capture, Ho risked several quick

trips into Hanoi to confer with ICP leaders. On one trip he was spotted by an informer, and the word flashed to the *Sûreté*. Dozens of police agents closed in swiftly from all directions. Ho's capture seemed inevitable.

Realizing that he was in a trap, Ho quickly stripped to the waist, changed places with a rickshaw driver pulling a passenger, and trotted off blithely through the cordon of police moving in on him from all sides.

The French crushed the uprising in Vinh. Many ICP leaders were seized, jailed and tortured. Ho himself, now in Hong Kong, was tried *in absentia* and sentenced to death by guillotine.

This news disturbed him far less than word that his father had died in western Cochin-China, a determined firebrand to the end, wandering about the country preaching revolt. Grieved, Ho vowed that his father should have a memorial one day in a revolutionary people's government.

In April 1931, a French Comintern agent, Joseph Ducroux, came to Hong Kong and found his way to Ho.

"He looked astonishingly thin and lithe," Ducroux reported. "He was clean-shaven at the time, apart from a few hairs on his upper lip. His face was sharp and seemed almost charred. . . . I've seldom met a human being who lived so frugally and was so disdainful of every comfort. . . . He had only one thought in his head—and it has, I think, obsessed him all his life long. His country. Vietnam. I won't say he wasn't a sincere internationalist, a true revolutionary. But to him, Vietnam has always come first."

British police, anxious about subversion in Hong Kong, arrested Ducroux. On June 6, at the urging of Inspector Arnoux, they also arrested Ho for extradition to Indo-

China to be executed for the Vinh uprising. But Sir Stafford Cripps, representing the British Anti-Imperialist League, defended Ho in court. He compelled the Hong Kong authorities to respect Ho's right to political asylum. Instead of extraditing Ho, they kept him in jail on their own charges.

In 1933 they revealed that the revolutionary known as Nguyen Ai-Quôc had died in prison of tuberculosis. In Hanoi Inspector Arnoux closed the *Sûreté* file on Ho with this notation. The news was reported in the Soviet press and in the Paris paper, *L'Humanité*. Grieved Vietnamese students in Moscow conducted a memorial service for him. Peasants mourned throughout Vietnam. They would never see Ho's like again.

Or . . . would they?

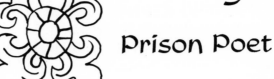

Prison Poet

REPORTS PERSISTED that Ho had been seen alive in Bangkok, Shanghai and Amoy. One rumor held that he had actually been set free secretly after agreeing to work for British Intelligence, and that news of his death had been issued as a cover-up. Another rumor said that in 1932 Ho had been transferred to a prison hospital because of a tubercular condition. British sympathizers had supposedly helped him escape by boat, smuggling him to Amoy and hiding him for six months until he was well enough to leave for Shanghai.

Whatever the truth, Ho was, indeed, very much alive, and in early 1933 Chinese Communists smuggled him aboard a Soviet liner. He was welcomed back in Moscow as the Comintern's leading expert on the theory and practice of Asian national revolution. Stalin, however, was somewhat suspicious.

Ho had always been something of a Communist maverick, putting the national interests of Vietnam before those of the Soviet Union. And his Marxist views of world revolution had been closer to those of Trotsky, who had been exiled for them. There was, besides, the possibility that the rumors of Ho's deal with British Intelligence were true.

So Stalin confined Ho to giving lectures on Vietnamese history at the Lenin Institute. The dictator's spies could report only one peculiar deviation about Ho's lectures— they were prepared and delivered to his classes in verse!

In 1936 the paranoiac Stalin began his infamous Moscow Trials, purging high Soviet leaders for "treason." Ho saw close friends arrested and convicted of crimes he knew they had not committed. It was an unsettling time for any Communist who had been on good terms with Trotsky and other critics of Stalin's policies.

"We cannot trust Ho," French Communist chief Maurice Thorez told Stalin. "He is a Trotskyite at heart."

But Ho somehow escaped arrest, perhaps because he had been shrewd enough to praise the writings of Stalin to a Comintern instructor he knew to be a Kremlin spy. In addition, Ho had been careful to take no sides in the ideological quarrels of leaders in the Politburo.

Ho found the Moscow Trials deeply disturbing, but still continued to believe that the Comintern offered him his best hope of overthrowing French colonialism in Indo-China. He grew worried, however, when world events began to shift Comintern thinking away from international revolution.

Communist agitation since the Russian Revolution had failed to overthrow capitalism anywhere else. It had, instead, only frightened the forces of ultra-conservatism into supporting Fascism. Their money had built the anti-Communist armies of Chiang Kai-shek in China, Mussolini in Italy, Hitler in Germany, and the warlords in Japan.

The threat of world Fascism alarmed Moscow in 1936 when the elected left-wing Loyalist government of Spain was attacked by the Spanish Fascists supported by Germany and Italy. The Comintern abandoned its tactics of promoting revolution in capitalist countries, calling instead for a United Front of Socialist and bourgeois forces opposed to Fascism.

Ho was dismayed. How could he be expected to cooperate with the very colonialism he was trying to overthrow, and which had sentenced him to death? But as a dutiful Communist, he rose in the Comintern to pledge Indo-Chinese support of the new policy as a temporary detour for anti-colonialism.

His painful reassignment of priorities was rewarded when the United Front succeeded in France. A new anti-Fascist Popular Front government was formed, headed by Ho's old comrade, Socialist Leon Blum. Pressure from Paris brought liberalization of colonial policy in Indo-China.

Political amnesty was granted to many of Ho's students and co-workers in Vietnamese prisons, among them his "favorite nephew," Pham Van Dong. The Indo-Chinese Communist party was given the right to operate openly. Communists were elected to the Saigon municipal council. And in 1938 a May Day parade, sponsored jointly by Socialists and Communists, brought tens of thousands of French and Vietnamese workers together in a stirring show of interracial unity.

Ho knew that these popular changes had not occurred because French colonial authorities had reformed, or were fully responsive to the wishes of Paris. The real reason was a grave new threat to their control of Indo-China, one they could not hope to fight off except with the support of the people—the threat of Japanese militarism.

Tokyo's armies were sweeping southward through China, aiming at mastery of all Asia, while the partner armies of the Rome-Berlin-Tokyo Axis sought to put Europe under Fascism. On July 11, 1938, Japanese forces even clashed with Soviet troops on the border of Manchuria. The Comintern saw the defense of China as vital to preventing world Fascism.

On orders from Moscow, Mao Tse-tung offered to ally his tough Chinese Red (Eighth Route) Army with Chiang's Nationalists in a joint struggle against the Japanese invaders. Chiang, his forces in disarray, quickly accepted.

The Comintern sent Ho to China in August to join Mao as a political commissar. Ho made his way through Japanese-held territory disguised as a beggar, pushing his belongings before him in a cart. By the time he reached Yenan, whose mud huts and mountain caves were the Red Army's bases in northeast China, he was weary and ill to the point of collapse.

It was several months before his health, always delicate at best from years of living as a prisoner and hunted refugee, was restored. Meanwhile his gentle ways won the admiration of the Chinese Reds, who began affectionately calling him "Uncle Ho," a term of endearment that persisted.

While in Yenan he may have married or taken a concubine, fathering a daughter who later became a Vietminh guerrilla fighter. But as with so many other rumors about his mysterious comings and goings during the 1930's, he was content neither to deny nor confirm the speculation.

When Ho had regained his health, Mao sent him to the south of China as political commissar under General Ying. Ho headed a liaison mission to train Chiang's troops in guerrilla tactics, as he had done eleven years earlier in Canton's Whampoa Military Academy before Chiang had turned against the Communists.

He would have preferred to be back in Vietnam working with his faithful disciple, Pham Van Dong, for the independence of his homeland. But, as he sighed to a French Communist friend, "I am a professional revolutionary. I am always on strict orders. My itinerary is always carefully prescribed—and you can't deviate from the route, can you?"

Meanwhile new world developments began influencing events in Indo-China. In 1939 Stalin suddenly signed a non-aggression pact with Hitler, hoping to turn Germany's armies away from the Soviet Union. The world United Front instantly crumbled as the Comintern ordered a halt to denunciations of Fascism, and outraged liberals denounced Russia's "pact with the devil." The governments of many countries began cracking down on local Communist parties.

The Indo-Chinese Communist party was once more declared illegal. Most of its leaders were seized and jailed. Pham Van Dong was one of those who escaped. In February 1940 he made his way to Yunnan Province in southern China to join his old instructor. Ho, now bearded and in European clothes with a soft felt hat, embraced his "favorite nephew" emotionally, tears in his eyes.

Accompanying Dong was pudgy Vo Nguyen Giap, the Communist leader in Tonkin, a former professor of French military history at the University of Hanoi. "He could draw every battle plan of Napoleon," one pupil recalled. Giap had learned his Marxism in France, like Ho, and had authored a manual for guerrilla fighters, *People's War, People's Army*.

Dong and Giap told Ho that the United Front was dead in Southeast Asia, and that the Communist party had been forced underground. Ho was not sorry; he had always suspected that the United Front was a policy designed by Moscow primarily to save the Soviet Union at the expense of world revolution. Now he was free once more to pursue the goal to which he was dedicated heart and soul—Vietnamese independence.

Dong and Giap became his principal deputies.

At Liuchow, Kwangsi Province, they established a base close to the Vietnamese border. Here they taught guerrilla tactics to Chinese Nationalists for use against the Japanese, and to young Vietnamese patriots for fighting the French.

Meanwhile England and France had gone to war with Nazi Germany, and France had been crushed with humiliating speed. On June 16, 1940, the Germans installed a puppet French government at Vichy under Marshal Henri-Philippe Pétain. Japan promptly dispatched a task force convoying troops to occupy French Indo-China. The French governor-general in Hanoi appealed to Washington for anti-aircraft guns and 120 planes to stand off the invasion.

Undersecretary of State Sumner Welles refused, explaining that a United States still at peace could not get involved militarily in Southeast Asia. When the frantic governor-general warned that without aid he would have to surrender, Welles replied, "It is what I would do in your place."

At that time Washington felt distinctly cool toward French colonialism in Indo-China, viewing the regime as a repressive one undeserving of any support.

On September 26 the Vichy government in France conceded control of Indo-China to the Japanese, who used the French administration in Hanoi as a puppet government. Nationalists, Communists, Socialists and liberals were hunted down and jailed. The country seethed with resentment.

"Now is the time," Ho told Dong and Giap thoughtfully.

In February 1941, after an eleven-year absence from his homeland, Ho slipped back across the Tonkin border, accompanied by his aides. Deeply moved by the occasion, Ho knelt on the Vietnamese side of the border and kissed the soil.

The three revolutionaries found an ideal "underground" headquarters in some limestone caves near Cao Bang that were well-concealed by tropical creepers and thickets. Ho named the mountain after Karl Marx, and dubbed an adjacent stream Lenin Creek.

On May 10 Communist leaders from all over Vietnam assembled secretly at Marx Mountain. Seated around a bamboo table in a hut built of branches, they listened to Ho Chi Minh's plans to free their country.

They must not, he told them, waste lives and energy in assassinations or acts of terrorism against the enemy. The primary goal was political education of the masses, organizing them solidly and secretly for the day when all would rise as one to throw off all foreign oppressors.

As Ho explained it, patriotism was the key that would eventually release the Vietnamese from their colonial prison. The Japanese, he was certain, would soon be driven out of Indo-China by the United States, which would not tolerate a Tokyo-dominated Pacific. America was not interested in becoming a colonial power, and would certainly not let French colonialism return. A power vacuum would therefore be created which could quickly be filled by the best-organized political party in Vietnam—one that was supported by the masses, and which had cooperated with the Americans.

Ho then astonished his listeners by telling them that the Indo-Chinese Communist party could not be that party. The ICP would be considered too radical by the Americans for such a role. He therefore proposed organizing a new patriotic organization—the League for the Independence of Vietnam, to be known popularly as the Vietminh ("United For Freedom"). Communists would organize it, but would be careful to keep in the background as it united all anti-colonial groups in a common struggle to liberate Vietnam.

The Central Committee of the ICP spent nine days discussing Ho's plan which, ironically, was a variant of the United Front idea he had opposed as not revolutionary enough. It was adopted on Ho's fifty-first birthday. To signify his own subordination of Communist goals to Vietnamese nationalism, the leader until then known chiefly as Nguyen Ai-Quôc changed his name to Ho Chi Minh ("He Who Enlightens").

Ho's new patriotic movement quickly became an effective underground opposition to the Japanese and Vichy French in Indo-China. As leader of the Vietminh, Ho won recognition and help from Free French forces in Vietnam who were secretly allied with de Gaulle's exile government in London, and from secret American OSS forces (Office of Strategic Services; now the CIA) in Southeast Asia.

The reaction in China, however, was hostile, reflecting in part centuries of traditional distrust between the two Asian peoples. Mao Tse-tung was outraged by what he considered a deviation from the Communist line, and a coolness sprang up between him and Ho. The Kuomintang was also irked because it was determined to create a Vietnamese independence movement that would owe its allegiance to Nationalist China. Chiang and the warlords did not want another Yenan flanking their southern border.

Late in 1941, when Ho returned to Liuchow to seek Kuomintang help, he was suddenly arrested by the local Nationalist warlord, General Chang Fa-kwei. Charged with being a "spy in the pay of the French," he was flung into jail. Word was sent back to Dong, who was running the Vietminh in Ho's absence, that Ho had died in prison.

"We were almost paralyzed with grief," Giap reported later. Funeral ceremonies were held at Marx Mountain.

But several months later when a newspaper came from China for Dong, a few lines of verse were found scribbled on the wrapper:

> The clouds are setting the peaks aglow,
> The peaks are hugging the clouds—
> I wander alone, roused to feeling,
> Scanning the distant southern sky:
> I am thinking of my friends.

"We were wild with joy, and no less astonished," Giap related. "The handwriting was Ho's!"

For fourteen months, bound to Chinese criminals by leg

irons and a yoke around his neck, Ho was shifted from one Chinese prison to another. After thirty such journeys he wrote wearily in the verse diary he kept with a bamboo brush, "With transfer after transfer the journey stretches out. I have had enough of this." His verses, he noted wistfully, were written with "tears for ink."

The guards were cruel, conditions primitive, rest impossible because of bedbugs and mosquitoes. Each prisoner was given half a basin of water daily. If he chose to wash he went without tea; if he had tea he went unwashed.

There were no mattresses or blankets in the dungeons. On cold nights prisoners shivered in misery on the ground until dawn. One morning when Ho awoke the prisoner sleeping against him proved to be dead. Ho wrote:

Through the endless nights, when sleep refuses to come,
I write more than a hundred poems on prison life.
At the end of each quatrain, I put down my brush,
And through the prison bars look up at the free sky.

There were periods of utter despair: "When shall I ever again enjoy days of freedom?" Dragged in irons along the road while guards carried pigs on their shoulders, Ho reflected ironically, "Once a man is forced to surrender his natural freedom, the value of a man is less than a pig."

Nevertheless he sought to endure his ordeal stoically: "In spite of being a prisoner, accused of being a spy, I move with all the dignity of an ancient government official." His time of trial, he believed, would strengthen him as a revolutionary: "Calamity has tempered and hardened me, and turned my mind to steel." He saw suffering as purifying:

The rice grain suffers under the blows of the pestle;
Yet admire its whiteness when the ordeal is over!

It is the same with humanity in our time;
To be a man you must endure the pounding of mis-
fortune.

He refused to allow the walls of his dungeons to imprison
his spirits: "It is your body which is in prison, not your
mind." The long journeys in leg-irons became less intoler-
able when he cast his eyes up instead of down:

Although they have tightly bound my arms and legs,
All over the mountain I can hear the songs of birds,
And inhale the forest perfume of spring flowers.
Who can prevent me from freely enjoying these?

He was filled with compassion for his fellow prisoners
who, like himself, were compelled to sleep in chains, and
saw a parallel with the workers and peasants of Indo-China
forced to chain themselves to colonialism for survival:

With hungry mouth open like a wicked monster
Each night the irons devour the legs of people. . . .
Yet there is one thing stranger in this world:
People rush to place their legs in irons.
Once they are shackled, they can sleep in peace.
Otherwise they would have no place to lay their heads.

Scoffing at poets who wrote only of natural beauty, Ho
insisted, "Today we should make poems including iron and
steel, and the poet also should know how to lead an attack."
He later told British correspondent James Cameron, "All
poets should have a spell in prison. It greatly composes the
mind!"

During his imprisonment the work of the Vietminh went
on in Vietnam under Dong and Giap. Dong confided to a
visiting French journalist, "We Communists are romantics,
too. You don't know how exciting it is to make a revolu-

tion!" In little more than a year the Vietminh became the only secret organization whose agents could move freely throughout the country with the full cooperation of the Vietnamese.

General Chang Fa-kwei, the warlord who had imprisoned Ho, created a rival organization called the Dong Minh Hoi under an old Vietnamese nationalist exile, Nguyen Hai Than. Chiang Kai-shek proposed to President Roosevelt that after World War II, Tonkin should become a Chinese trusteeship under Than. But the Kuomintang soon realized that only the Vietminh enjoyed popular support throughout Vietnam, with an effective network of spies and plotters in both the Japanese and French strongholds.

Late in 1942 Chang Fa-kwei sent for Ho. Without telling Chiang Kai-shek, he offered the imprisoned revolutionary his freedom if he would agree to supply copies of Vietminh intelligence reports on the French and Japanese to the Kuomintang. Ho would also receive one hundred thousand dollars a month to help the Vietminh sabotage the Japanese. Ho promptly agreed.

His return to the cave headquarters at Marx Mountain was greeted with astonishment and joy by Dong and Giap.

All through 1942 and 1943 their guerrilla forces, trained at a war college in Liuchow, grew in numbers and skill. Ho and Dong coordinated Vietminh political strategy, while Giap directed hit-and-run raids against the enraged troops of the Japanese and Vichy French. Pursued, the freedom fighters simply melted away into the peasant masses.

Ho was shocked in December 1943 when General Charles de Gaulle, speaking in Algiers, revealed that the

Free French intended to re-establish French authority in Indo-China once the Japanese had been driven out. The Vietminh had been collaborating with Gaullists in Vietnam against the Japanese and Vichy French, under the illusion that the Free French would agree to independence for Vietnam. If De Gaulle imagined that Ho was struggling against the Japanese only to restore French colonialism, Ho assured Dong that *Le Grand Charles* was in for an unpleasant surprise!

In March 1944 General Chang Fa-kwei summoned all Vietnamese freedom factions, including the Vietminh, to Liuchow. He told the assembled delegates that it was time for them to choose a provisional government to take power after Vietnam was liberated. Ho was stunned when a pro-Chinese Vietnamese was selected as premier, and he was only named one among many ministers. If De Gaulle saw postwar Vietnam as French once more, the Kuomintang obviously saw it as a Chinese satellite.

Ho was determined that it would be neither. He simply ignored Chang Fa-kwei's provisional government, and it faded into oblivion for lack of popular support. Only Ho and the Vietminh continued to be trusted by the people to bring about a free Vietnam for the Vietnamese.

In July Giap came to the Marx Mountain headquarters, urging Ho to call for an armed insurrection throughout northern Vietnam. The time, he insisted, was ripe. But Ho counseled patience. He did not want to waste lives or the strength of the Vietminh against a militarily superior enemy.

As Ho saw the shape of coming events, the fall of Germany would release America's full might in the Pacific.

With the Chinese the Americans would begin invading Indo-
China. The Japanese military would probably declare mar-
tial law, shoving aside the Vichy French. The Gaullists
would rise, seeking to beat the Americans and Chinese to
the control of Hanoi.

"Indo-China will be reduced to anarchy," Ho prophe-
sied. "We shall not even need to seize power, for there will
be no power." Gaullists, Americans and Chinese would
then discover that the Vietminh had already waged and
won a "peaceful revolution" in Vietnam, with the people
behind them. If a general insurrection became necessary,
the Vietminh would have the guerrilla army, the plans,
communications and popular support to enforce independence.

Ho did not know it at the time, but he had a powerful
ally against the French on his side—the president of the
United States.

Fighting the Japanese

"INDO-CHINA SHOULD NOT GO BACK to France but . . . be administered by an international trusteeship," Franklin D. Roosevelt wrote to Secretary of State Cordell Hull in 1944. "France has had the country—30 million inhabitants—for nearly 100 years, and the people are worse off than they were at the beginning. . . . France has milked it for 100 years. The people of Indo-China are entitled to something better than that."

At the Yalta Conference in February 1945 Roosevelt sounded out China's aspirations in Indo-China. Chiang Kai-shek sought to disarm him by replying, "We don't want it. They are not Chinese. They would not assimilate into the Chinese people." He shrugged agreement to FDR's plan to put Indo-China under a UN trusteeship. Stalin agreed, but Winston Churchill fumed, "Nonsense!" Roosevelt laughed and called him "a prejudiced old imperialist."

As American air power began to strike at Japanese bases in Indo-China in late 1944, Giap organized secret Vietminh military bases. Guerrilla attacks against the Japanese were supported by Gaullist units who deserted from Vichy garrisons.

The Vietminh were fed, sheltered and hidden by villagers wherever they fought. The Vichy French struck back that winter by depriving of food stores villages in areas under Vietminh control, causing widespread starvation.

Ho decided to ask the Americans for arms and ammunition. Making a secret trip to Kunming, he found his way to the American OSS.

In exchange for help, he offered to supply the OSS with intelligence, sabotage Japanese units, and help rescue Allied pilots shot down over Vietnam. The OSS forwarded his proposal to Washington. While waiting for an answer, Ho agreed to help the United States Office of War Information by translating and interpreting important captured enemy documents.

The State Department was reluctant to get involved with Ho. As the leading Communist in Southeast Asia, he was anathema to America's most important Asian ally, Chiang Kai-shek. Ho also refused to pledge that he would use American arms given him against only the Japanese, not against the French. That, too, could become a sticky issue with another important ally, De Gaulle. But Ho agreed to admit teams of OSS agents parachuted into areas under his control.

On March 9 Roosevelt personally directed the OSS to give Ho some sidearms and light weapons. One month later the president died. His plans for Indo-China died with him.

The small supply of OSS arms mattered less to Ho than

his success in becoming an American ally. It was on American support that he was building his hopes of keeping foreign hands off Vietnam when he was able to free it.

For the bulk of Vietminh arms Ho relied on weapons captured from the Japanese and Vichy French by Giap's raids, and on American arms bought from Chinese warlords. The steadily-growing "people's army" now consisted of crack, tough guerrilla units that fought with fanatical patriotism.

On March 9 the Japanese, exasperated by the inability of the Vichy French to cope with the Vietminh, fulfilled Ho's predictions by abruptly taking over the government themselves. Thousands of French officials were jailed. Many fled to China; others joined the Gaullist units.

The Japanese command set up Bao Dai, emperor of Annam, as head of a puppet "independent" Indo-China. Now Giap urged Ho to call for a general uprising against the Japanese. But Ho felt that it would be safer first to weaken and confuse them by a series of local revolts, timed to keep their troops rushing from one part of Vietnam to another.

Giap moved his forces into position. Then local insurrections began exploding like sputtering firecrackers all over Vietnam. The enraged Japanese unleashed a savage reign of terror. Thousands of suspected Vietminh, along with French prisoners, were brutally massacred.

An American with the OSS, identified only as "Lieutenant John," was parachuted into the Vietminh enclave in the jungles of Tonkin. His mission was to establish an underground to help Allied prisoners of the Japanese escape. Vietminh scouts led him to Ho's secret command post, a

camp of four huts in a tiny valley near the village of Kim
Lung, set in the dense rain forest of a mountainside.

John found the fifty-five-year-old Vietnamese leader
seriously ill of an undefined tropical fever. Ho lay helpless
on a hut floor, little more than a skeleton, glassy-eyed and
trembling violently. In a coma for hours on end, he refused
to die, stubbornly fighting to remain conscious.

During one of his lucid periods he whispered to Giap,
"Now circumstances are in our favor. Independence must
be grasped at all costs, even if you must set the mountains
afire. As upheaval grows, we must take advantage of it and
broaden our bases to increase popular support."

"I realized," Giap wrote later, "that he felt so weak that
he was dictating his last instructions to me."

John set up his portable short-wave radio, directing the
first eight-man OSS rescue and sabotage team that parachuted into Vietnam behind Japanese lines. The arrival of
the Americans saved Ho's life. They were amazed at the
sight of the emaciated little figure with a long, scraggly
goatee on his bone-sharp chin. Could this pathetic creature
really be the legendary Ho Chi Minh?

The medic of the team, recognizing that Ho was on the
verge of death, gave him emergency treatment with qui-
nine, sulfa and other "miracle" drugs. He was frankly as
astonished as Ho's overjoyed lieutenants when, ten days
later, Ho was back on his feet, miraculously recovered.

The French who had been working with the OSS had
warned the Americans that Ho was a dangerous Communist—cunning, ruthless, fearless, sly, not to be trusted. But
the little Vietnamese in a long-sleeved white shirt, with
khaki shorts that exposed his matchstick legs and knobby

knees, impressed them as far more of a Gandhi than a Stalin.

All the OSS teams who came in contact with him had nothing but affectionate praise for "Uncle Ho," whose gentle charm led them all to agree that he was, as one OSS officer put it "an awfully sweet guy." They considered him a dedicated nationalist first, and a Marxist only incidentally.

Giap was considered a much more rigid hard-liner. The Vietminh general's burning black eyes gave him a grim, angry look that made believable a statement attributed to him: "The Russian Revolution cost two million lives, so we can certainly sacrifice half a million people."

Units of the two hundred picked guerrillas in Ho's camp guided, fed and fought beside the OSS commandos, aiding in the rescue of seventeen Allied fliers shot down in the jungle. Ho's intelligence reports, relayed over Lt. John's short-wave radio, also proved invaluable in pin-pointing Japanese targets for bombing. His intelligence network astounded the Americans.

Once an OSS team brought with them a French army captain, passing him off to Ho as an American officer. Although the Frenchman kept his mouth shut through several hours of conference, Ho finally pointed a finger at him and said quietly, "This man is not an American." They assured him he was wrong.

"Look, who are you guys trying to kid?" he replied dryly in the American slang he had picked up. "This man is not part of the deal." He amazed them by citing the French officer's name, rank and station in China, indicating that the Vietminh had eyes and ears everywhere.

The Frenchman was politely but firmly escorted back to

the Chinese border by Vietminh guerrillas. One OSS officer expressed surprise that Ho had let him go, since he would carry back with him the location of Ho's headquarters.

"It will be interesting to hear the French reaction," Ho shrugged. "Perhaps they will not think of me as a murderous bandit." Instead of upbraiding the newly arrived Americans for their attempt to deceive him, he prepared a feast for them of jungle deer and stewed tiger liver. Ho's contacts with the OSS had deepened his liking for Americans, and his admiration for American ideals.

Lt. John was astonished one day when Ho asked him to recite the American Declaration of Independence. Ho explained that he wanted to write such a declaration for Vietnam. John admitted that he didn't know the words, but gave Ho the gist of what the Declaration said. Ho made notes and used them in writing his own declaration for Vietnam, in preparation for the day when he could proclaim his country free.

As the Japanese empire of conquest in the Pacific began to crumble, Ho was alarmed by reports from his spies in China that Chiang Kai-shek was planning to annex Tonkin after the war. Through Lt. John he sent out secret messages to an old French friend, now with the De Gaulle forces in France, urging that the Free French send a mission to Ho to work out plans for joint resistance to a Chinese take-over.

"If it weren't for the war, of course," one OSS officer later said, "Ho wouldn't have had a chance against the grip of French colonialism. He was afraid of Chinese help because he knew they'd demand their pound of flesh for it. That was why I think he was ready to remain pro-West."

De Gaulle, who had no intention of letting Indo-China slip through his fingers to the Vietminh, nevertheless recognized the importance of working with Ho to keep the Chinese out. In April 1945, with the approaching end of World War II signaled by Hitler's suicide in Berlin and the organization of the UN at San Francisco, De Gaulle sent a French mission headed by Jean Sainteny to Ho's jungle headquarters.

Sainteny demanded that Ho agree to let the French return to Indo-China after the war. Ho protested, but finally consented if the French guaranteed total independence for a united Vietnam within five to ten years. The French diplomat cautiously agreed to future negotiations on that point.

He confided to Ho that the French were actually far more worried that the Americans, rather than the Chinese, would seek to replace them in Indo-China. Sainteny's mission came to nothing when De Gaulle decided to keep Vietnam divided in three parts, the better to assure French rule.

Frustrated, Ho appealed to Washington for support and help against both the French and the Chinese. But now there was a new president in the White House. Harry S. Truman rapidly embraced a new, rigid anti-Communist foreign policy. Ho's appeal was spurned as Washington threw its support behind Chiang's right-wing regime in China, and a return of the French to Indo-China. Ho was grieved.

"If you do not help us achieve our goal," he hinted to the OSS, "I know a country that will be only too glad to come to our aid." But no one realized better than Ho that the

Soviet Union was too far away and war-ravaged to be of real help. All he could hope was that events would change Washington's mind.

When the atomic bombs were dropped on Hiroshima and Nagasaki early in August, Ho knew that Japan's surrender was imminent. Calling all Vietnam political factions to an emergency meeting in Tan Trao, north of Hanoi, on August 10, he warned the sixty delegates that it was imperative to form a united front at once. Only in that way could they all confront Allied forces, invading to take over from the Japanese, with the *fait accompli* of a nationalist government in power.

Three days later they formed a National Liberation Committee to wrest control from the Japanese military in all parts of the country. The delegates sped back to their local regions to coordinate operations with the Vietminh.

Then, at last, Ho Chi Minh issued the long-awaited call to his people for a national uprising.

"Unite around the National Liberation Committee, our provisional government at present," he urged. "See that its policies and orders are carried out throughout the country. By this means our fatherland will surely win independence —and our people will surely soon win their freedom!"

Japan capitulated to the United States on August 14. Next day the Japanese in Hanoi handed over the government to Emperor Bao Dai, thus avoiding the humiliation of surrendering Indo-China to either the Americans or the French.

But the Vietnamese were in no mood to settle for an imperial government. Tens of thousands demonstrated angrily. By August 19 there was a full-scale insurrection, and a day later the Vietminh was in full control of Tonkin and Annam. Ho immediately gave orders to break camp, and set out on a long march to Hanoi with his headquarters forces.

"On the way, I got my first glimpse of Ho's ruthlessness," reported French correspondent Jean Lacouture. "His troops would range ahead of us, and often we would come into a burned village. Ho told us the villagers had burned their own homes to prevent the Japanese from using them, but we did not believe him. We knew that this was his way of getting 'cooperation' from an area. A couple of matches, a few bullets, and the people were on his side."

But Lacouture also saw the other side of Ho as he liberated villages along the march that had been starving under the Japanese. The painfully thin Vietminh leader distributed his unit's meager supplies of rice—including his own rations—to the children, women, and elderly.

"How can I eat when so many of my people are hungry!" he said, waving aside protests of his worried aides. He also sought out a literate person—if there was one—in each village, assigning him the task of teaching another to read, then both teaching others, and so on until the village was literate.

Ho and his entourage reached the environs of Hanoi at the end of August. They were driven in open cars and trucks along pleasant tree-lined avenues and parks to the Governor's Palace. Pretty girls in gossamer *ao dai* gowns, and workers in black trousers and tightly-buttoned white jackets, gave Ho a thunderous ovation. OSS men accompanying him also received a tumultuous welcome.

Ho was greeted at the palace by Emperor Bao Dai, who

promptly assured the little revolutionist that he intended to abdicate his throne in favor of the Vietminh, and would be glad to serve Ho as "Supreme Political Advisor." Ho accepted the offer diplomatically, letting Bao Dai save face while acquiring monarchial recognition of his new government. Word came from Cochin-China that the south was also in Vietminh hands, giving Ho control of the whole country.

Now the long years of his exile, imprisonment, poverty, and suffering had been redeemed at last, his dream come true. All power lay in Ho's grasp. Should he use it to create a national democratic government representing all the coalition forces he had united in the National Liberation Committee? Or should he establish a Communist Vietnam —the goal for which he had been educated, trained and supported by the Comintern?

"During the few months I was in Hanoi as Supreme Councilor," Emperor Bao Dai said later, "I saw Ho Chi Minh suffer. He was fighting a battle within himself. . . . He realized Communism was not best for our country, but it was too late. He could not overcome his allegiance to Communism."

To judge the accuracy of this view, its source must be considered. Bao Dai, a monarch ousted from power by a revolutionary, had also been dismissed as Ho's advisor a few months later. But prejudiced or not, Bao Dai's view of Ho was to prove highly important in influencing American foreign policy.

On September 2, 1945, Ho proclaimed the establishment of a Democratic Republic of Vietnam. When he read the Declaration of Independence he had written for his country to a wildly cheering crowd of half a million in Hanoi, he had Thomas Jefferson, not Karl Marx, in mind.

"All men are created equal," Ho declared. "They are endowed by their Creator with certain unalienable rights, that among these are life, liberty and the pursuit of happiness. This immortal statement was made in the Declaration of Independence of the United States of America in 1776. In a broader sense this means all the people of the earth are equal from birth, all . . . have a right to live, to be happy and free."

The principle of self-determination adopted by the UN at San Francisco, Ho pointed out, entitled Vietnam to independence: "A people who have courageously opposed French domination for more than eighty years, a people who have fought side by side with the Allies against the Fascists during these last years—such a people must be free and independent."

Ho denounced French imperalists for having besmirched their own heritage of liberty, equality and fraternity by their inhuman rule in Vietnam, and charged them with dividing the country into three parts to prevent national unity.

"They have built more prisons than schools," he cried. "They have mercilessly slain our patriots; they have drowned our uprisings in rivers of blood. . . . To weaken our race they have forced us to use opium and alcohol. . . . They have fleeced us to the backbone, impoverished our people, and devastated our land. They have robbed us of our rice fields, our mines, our forests, and our raw materials. . . . The whole Vietnamese people, animated by a common purpose, are determined to fight to the bitter end against any attempt by the French colonialists to reconquer our country!"

The Vietminh declared Ho provisional president of the new republic, with Dong as his minister of finance and Giap as his minister of defense. National elections were announced for January 6, 1946, over the objections of Giap. He saw no sense in risking the power they had fought so long and so hard to win, or in diluting their control of the country by sharing it with anti-Vietminh politicians.

But Ho had changed his mind about elections. He wanted to prove to France, the United States and the UN that he and his government represented the free choice of the Vietnamese people. There could be no doubt about the outcome of elections. Ho was the most popular national figure in the nation, the Vietminh the most respected party.

Paris and Washington professed to believe in democracy. Then how could they possibly deny it to the Vietnamese?

Ho, Dong and Giap took up residence in the Puginier Palace, where they had been preceded by a dozen French governor-generals. But Ho chose to live in a modest little cottage at the rear of the palace that had formerly been servants' quarters. Greeting visitors in sandals and a peasant tunic, he presented a striking contrast to the palace reception room with its crystal chandeliers, fine parquet floor, rich Brussels carpet, and Louis XIV sofas. Ho secretly enjoyed looking out of place in such sumptuous surroundings.

Ho's unmarried sister, Thanh, who was now living in a village in Annam, was astonished when she saw a picture of the new president in a newspaper. He bore an amazing resemblance to her younger brother, Nguyen Van Thanh, despite all the years since she had last seen him. Could it be possible that, somehow, he was the world-famous Ho Chi Minh?

She set out for the Puginier Palace at Hanoi carrying a gift of ducks and duck eggs for the new president who had freed their country, whether he was her brother or not.

When Ho heard who was asking to see him, he swept aside all state business and received her with open arms. They wept quietly, moved by profound joy as they embraced.

During the time they were together Ho told Thanh of all that had happened to him since he had left home, a youth of twenty-two. They compared their experiences in prison as revolutionaries, and rejoiced that their sacrifices had borne fruit.

Some five years later, when Thanh sent Ho word that their brother Khiem had died, Vietnam was once more war-torn. From a jungle outpost Ho sent a message mourning his inability to attend the funeral: "I humbly apologize for this failure in brotherly devotion, and beg to be forgiven as one who has to put affairs of state before family feelings."

Ho's deep respect for the family unit, and his understanding of how important it was to the Vietnamese, was indicated by the nature of his first major message as chief of state. It was addressed to all the children of the country—Vietnam's future—and was written in the sugary, sentimental style of a typical doting uncle:

> My dear children. . . . Today is the mid-autumn festival. Your parents have bought you lanterns, tambourines, crackers, flowers and lots of other toys. . . . You are

rejoicing, and your Uncle Ho rejoices with you. Do you know why? First because I love you very much. Second, because last year . . . our country was still living under oppression and you, my children, were still little slaves. . . . Today, enjoy yourselves as much as you like. Tomorrow, I hope you will give your minds to your studies. . . . This year I have no present for you. I just send you my loving kisses.

For most Vietnamese parents, that was enough.

"I Swear I Have Not Betrayed You!"

JEAN SAINTENY, De Gaulle's representative in Vietnam, was back in Hanoi. He had arrived just before the Japanese surrender, hoping to induce the Japanese to turn Hanoi over to the French. But they, preferring Vietnam in Asian rather than Western hands, simply held him in protective custody in the Hotel Metropole. When the Vietminh took control of Hanoi, they continued Sainteny's isolation while they organized the new republic and consolidated their power.

Ho held off seeing him because of continued hope that recognition and support for the Vietminh would come, however grudgingly, from the United States. Ho's wartime cooperation with the OSS had won the highest praise of the American officers who had worked with him. When OSS Major Archimedes Patti, in charge of liberating war prisoners, flew to Hanoi, he made no secret of his open support of Ho's regime.

Sainteny fumed at reports that Patti was promising Ho

arms to prevent any French attempt to overturn the new republic. He was caustic about the Americans' "infantile anti-colonialism, which blinded most of them." But one U.S. officer in Hanoi saw any other position as unrealistic.

"Ho was totally intractable," he declared. "I doubt that there was ever any way in which Ho could be dealt with. He had only one dream, and that was the freedom of Vietnam."

Americans who came to Hanoi from the China Combat Command were also sympathetic to the cause of the frail, gentle liberator of his people. They joined the OSS men in a Vietnam-American Friendship Association. One meeting was attended by General Giap, who wanted to show his respect for the Americans. As "The Star-Spangled Banner" was played, he saluted the only way he knew how—with a clenched fist.

The French received support for their claims from the British, who opposed an anti-colonial Vietnam as an inflammatory example to their own Asian colonies. The Free French, moreover, had been part of the victorious Allied team that had defeated Fascism. De Gaulle insisted that his war allies were obligated to protect French legal rights in Indo-China.

British occupation forces had been assigned the task of accepting the surrender of Cochin-China from the Japanese in the south. Less than three weeks after Ho had proclaimed a united Republic of Vietnam, the British released and rearmed five thousand interned French troops. Their combined forces "restored order" by attacking Saigon and seizing it from the Vietminh as Paris rushed fifty thousand reinforcements.

These developments, unopposed by either the UN or the
United States, were the beginning of the long series of tragic
episodes that became the explosive, complex Vietnam War
which would shake France and polarize America during the
next quarter of a century. Ho warned grimly, "If the United
Nations forget their solemn promise and don't grant Indo-
China full independence, we will keep on fighting until we
get it."

One night he gave a diplomatic dinner at the governor's
palace, inviting OSS Major Frank White. It was not lost on
the French, British and Chinese diplomats present that they
were placed furthest from Ho, while White sat beside
him.

"Mr. President," the American whispered, "I think that
there is some resentment over the seating arrangement."

"I see that," Ho smiled. "But who else could I talk
to?"

Sainteny was convinced that France could reach an
amicable settlement with Ho, whom he greatly admired.

"From my first dealings with Ho Chi Minh," he wrote, "I
derived the impression that this ascetic man, whose face
reflected a mixture of intelligence, guile and subtlety, was a
person of the highest caliber. . . . His intelligence, vast culture, unbelievable energy and total unselfishness had earned
him unparalleled prestige and popularity in the eyes of his
people. His talk, his deeds, his bearing—everything about
him served to convince one that a solution by force of arms
was repugnant to him."

The Chinese pressed their support on Ho, but he avoided
their embrace as diplomatically as he could. The French
had permitted two hundred thousand Chinese Nationalist

troops to fan out through Tonkin at the war's end, presumably to supervise the departure of the Japanese. Instead they had pillaged the villages, seized land to settle on, and threatened northern Tonkin with economic collapse. Ho planned to insist that the French get rid of the Chinese as part of any settlement.

"I prefer to endure the sewer smell of French colonialism for five more years," he told Giap frankly, "than smell the Chinese variety for the rest of my life." Knowledge of the countless times his ancestors had had to drive the Chinese out of their country made Ho determined not to allow them to stay a moment longer than he had to.

If the Americans refused to champion his cause, he knew, he would have little choice but to work out some kind of accommodation with the French. In that case he counted on help from Maurice Thorez, the Comintern leader who was now deputy premier of the new Free French government. When Ho's minister of propaganda, Tran Huy Lieu, organized a violently anti-French demonstration on the streets of Hanoi, Ho reproached him openly at a cabinet meeting.

"All right, so it's fun abusing the colonialists," he shrugged. "But where does it get you?"

In preparation for the nationwide elections on January 6, 1946, Ho officially disbanded the Indo-China Communist party as a gesture of national unity. He was presented to voters only as the famous nationalist hero of the Vietminh. But five years later he admitted, "The Party proclaimed its dissolution, but in fact went underground, continuing to direct the state and the people." The distinction was largely a semantic one, since it was no secret that Ho, the Vietminh, and the ICP were largely commingled.

Ho's enormous popularity and prestige assured his victory at the polls. He defeated all rivals by an overwhelming majority, and in the new national assembly, Vietminh leaders captured 230 of the 300 seats. The election was observed by Donald Lancaster, a former political officer in the Saigon British legation. He reported that there was free and full voting throughout Tonkin and Annam. In French-held Cochin-China, however, the Vietminh were able to hold elections only in areas under their control.

Lancaster criticized "some evidence of a readiness to fabricate returns; nevertheless, the results, which gave the Vietminh a clear majority in the assembly, were probably fairly indicative of the state of public opinion at that time."

The elections created the first independent Vietnamese government in eighty years, and the first one in a thousand years that was a republic. But it was a republic in deep trouble.

Some members of Ho's cabinet insisted that he had no alternative but to turn for help to Chiang Kai-shek, as a fellow Asian opposed to Western colonialism. But Ho reminded them how often their ancestors had had to fight to break the smothering embrace of the Chinese.

He still pinned his hopes on American aid. But De Gaulle had introduced Emperor Bao Dai, now in Europe, to William C. Bullitt, former Ambassador to France, whose views had great influence in the State Department. Bao Dai convinced Bullitt that Ho and the Vietminh were puppets of Mao Tse-tung and the Chinese Reds, part of a plot to put all Southeast Asia under Communist control.

This concept later served as the basis for Secretary of State John Foster Dulles' "domino theory," which held that if one Indo-Chinese country was allowed to go Communist, it would tumble every adjacent country into the Communist orbit, with grave consequences for American interests in the Pacific and Asia. Bao Dai's version of Vietnam affairs, endorsed by Bullitt, strongly influenced United States policy.

"The United States became a status quo power, afraid of change anywhere in the world for fear that change might lead to 'Godless Communism,' " noted James P. Warburg, the Wall Street industrialist commended by four American presidents for his work on behalf of international peace. "In appointing itself the global guardian against communism, the United States lost touch with the rising tide of nationalism and, by failure to befriend nationalism, became its enemy, allowing the two great communist powers to identify with the emerging peoples and to assume a spurious role as their protectors."

President Truman remained silent while France reestablished its colonial presence in Indo-China. There were other reasons besides the Bao Dai/Bullitt report.

At the end of the war the Western allies secretly agreed to divide up spheres of influence in Asia. The United States was granted control of China, Japan, the Philippines, and other central and northern Pacific countries. The Indian Ocean area was put under British power. France was given control of her old colonial empire in Indo-China. Each agreed to support the other's sphere of influence.

The United States also had economic reasons to want Indo-China kept in "reliable" hands. There were American mining and oil investments in Vietnam, and geologists' reports suspected vast rich underwater oil fields off the coast of Indo-China. President Eisenhower later admitted, "The loss of Vietnam . . . would have spelled the loss of valuable deposits of tin, and prodigious supplies of rubber and rice."

Curiously, in Truman's two-volume autobiography, which ended with the year 1952, there is not a single mention of either Ho Chi Minh or the Republic of Vietnam.

Still hoping that Washington would come to his rescue, Ho sought to delay coming to terms with his old enemy, France. But time was running out. French General Jean Leclerc set sail from Saigon with a convoy of troops, and the French fleet had pulled into the Gulf of Tonkin.

As Hanoi was threatened with siege, Ho told French correspondent P. M. Dessinges, "We feel no hatred whatever for France and the French people. Neither of us should let other countries tell us what we ought and ought not to do. We must reach a settlement. But mark my words—if we are forced to fight, we are determined to fight to the end!"

On March 6, 1946, he met with Sainteny aboard a French cruiser to negotiate an agreement. Ho won French recognition of his Democratic Republic of Vietnam, but only as a "free state within the French Union." Control of Cochin-China, including Saigon, was left to future negotiations. Ho also agreed that French troops could remain in Vietnam for five years, on condition that they "relieve" the Nationalist Chinese troops there—that is, force them to leave.

Expressing disappointment at the concessions he had been forced to make, Ho nevertheless embraced Sainteny and told him, "Our friendship is my one consolation."

His concessions disgruntled Giap, the Marxist faction in

Ho's cabinet, and the people of Vietnam. They wanted the French removed completely. But Ho knew that his weak government could not resist the French military. He also told Sainteny, "While we want to govern ourselves, I need your professional men, your engineers and your capital."

Ho's political rivals began circulating rumors that he had "sold out" to the French. To allay widespread discontent, Ho called a huge mass meeting in Hanoi's Place du Théâtre. He explained why he had made concessions to the French and asked, "Why sacrifice fifty to one hundred thousand men when we can achieve independence through negotiation, perhaps within five years?"

In a voice choked with emotion, the frail figure with the familiar wispy tuft of chin hair vowed, "I, Ho Chi Minh, have always led you along the path of freedom. I have spent my whole life fighting for our country's independence. You know I would sooner die than betray the nation. I swear I have not betrayed you!"

His eyes filled with tears as his people gave him a roaring, deafening ovation that refused to stop.

But fresh trouble was in store for the Ho-Sainteny accords. France was teetering on the verge of bankruptcy as a result of postwar shortages, black markets, inflation, and strikes. Governments composed of unstable coalitions rose and fell in quick succession. As a result, Indo-Chinese affairs were left in the hands of the ministry of colonies, a bureaucracy staffed by reactionary colonialists. They disapproved of the Hanoi Agreement and violated it.

Taking control of all Cochin-China, despite furious local resistance, they insisted that by signing the pact Ho had put all of Vietnam under French direction.

"It is certainly regrettable that France minimized this man," Sainteny later said ruefully, "and was unable to understand his value and the power at his disposal."

Ho drafted a constitution for the new republic. Basing it largely on the American Constitution, he pointedly proclaimed the nation of Vietnam "an indivisible whole."

Then on May 30, 1946, he led a delegation to Paris to insist that the French government honor its word.

En route, Ho heard a radio report that the new French high commissioner in Indo-China, Admiral Thierry d'Argenlieu, had proclaimed a separate "Republic of Cochin-China." General Douglas MacArthur, commenting from Tokyo, denounced the French move as "an ignoble betrayal." Ho was stunned.

He recognized the timing of D'Argenlieu's proclamation as an attempt to sabotage his mission. The *fait accompli* defied both the Hanoi Agreement and Ho's insistence upon a united, free Vietnam. He was deeply worried. Would the hotheads in his cabinet respond by ordering attacks on the French?

Sainteny met Ho's plane at Biarritz and flew with him to Paris. Ho complained bitterly of D'Argenlieu's treachery. Sainteny assured him that the whole mess would be straightened out by the newly-elected premier, Georges Bidault.

The Bidault government gave Ho a warm official welcome at Le Bourget airport, flying the Vietnamese flag alongside the French tricolor. He was given a suite at the Royal-Monceau Hotel near the Place de l'Etoile. A red carpet running from the sidewalk to his door indicated political recognition of him as a chief of state.

Jewish and Algerian leaders of independence movements were also quartered at the Royal-Monceau. Ho met and became friendly with David Ben-Gurion, whose description of the Jewish struggle for an independent homeland moved Ho to invite him to set up an Israeli government-in-exile in Hanoi.

As the summer wore on, Ho's hope of forcing France to honor the Hanoi Agreement grew increasingly dim. His losing battle could be gauged, Ben-Gurion told him dryly, by the progressive shrinkage of his red carpet—first back to the lobby, then to the staircase, finally only to the corridor in front of his suite. Ho nevertheless continued to do everything he could think of to win over the French.

Enormously popular, he was in demand at all levels of Paris life. Friends from his old Paris days sought him out eagerly, taking him to their old haunts. Leaders of French society were charmed by the quiet dignity, subtle wit and modesty of the little Asian who always wore a shabby, high-buttoned linen work tunic to all occasions, however grand.

In meetings with Bidault, Ho would embrace him hopefully as a friend. "Bidault wasn't too keen on such gestures," laughed a French aide, "because of Uncle Ho's goatee."

The press compared Ho to a doting grandfather, to Confucius, Buddha, and Gandhi. His shrewd flair for public relations kept him and the Vietnamese cause in the headlines. He encouraged interviews by presenting roses to girl reporters, and by signing his name in blood for male correspondents.

He was always good for a human interest story. Invited to an official reception at the Paris town hall, he declined all refreshments but finally, to the amazement of Bidault, put an apple in his pocket as he left and presented it fondly to a little girl outside.

One reporter asked him why he was a Marxist, and why he hadn't introduced Marxism into the Vietnam Republic.

"Everyone has the right to his own doctrine," Ho replied. "I studied and chose Marx. Jesus said two thousand years ago that one should love one's enemies. That dogma has not yet been realized. When will Marxism be possible in Vietnam, where production is low? Who can say? Remember that I have been President only a few brief months. Until then I had been forced to spend my entire life in hiding."

He was upset when an open letter to him appeared in the Paris press, written by some Vietnamese Marxists in Paris:

"We are the remnants of the handful of men trained by you in 1925. Your ideas made a deep impression upon us. We saw you as the symbol of all young workers in Vietnam. Yet you have signed an agreement with the French to accept self-government, not independence. The strength of our faith in you, in the days when your name stood for the great revolutionary idea, is equaled today by the rage in our hearts. We are ashamed that we should have chosen the wrong elder!"

Deeply distressed, Ho invited his disillusioned expatriate followers to his hotel suite. He explained to them that if he had not submerged the Communist party and compromised with the French, the Kuomintang troops occupying northern Tonkin would have made all hopes of independence impossible. His critics were impressed, but left still doubting that Ho's trust of the French had been wise.

Their skepticism was being reflected by the Marxists in Hanoi, who were further enraged by D'Argenlieu when he called a conference in Saigon to work out a new Indo-Chinese Federation consisting of Cochin-China, Laos and Cambodia—in effect, France's old colony minus Tonkin and Annam. Vietminh militants talked of replacing Ho with Giap, and throwing the French out of Vietnam once and for all.

French General Salan warned Ho that it might be dangerous to leave the republic in the hands of young hotheads like Giap and Truong Chinh any longer. Ho professed not to be worried: "What could they possibly do without me? It was I who made them." But Sainteny joined with Salan in urging him to return to Hanoi as quickly as possible.

Then Ho played his trump card. "What would I be able to do if I went home empty-handed?" he pointed out. "Arm me against the extremists who want to displace me, and you will not regret it. *Honor our agreement!* If you don't, we will have to fight you. You will kill ten of our men and we will kill one of yours. But in the end it will be the French, and not us, who will tire of it!"

Fighting the French

SAINTENY PLEADED HO'S CASE to the French government, but to no avail. On September 16, 1946, Ho had a last-ditch negotiating session lasting until long after midnight with Overseas Minister Marius Moutet, an old friend of his early Paris days. Moutet stubbornly defended French interests.

Ho was forced to sign a *modus vivendi* (working compromise) that validated the Hanoi Agreement with Sainteny, but established "democratic freedom" for Cochin-China with an end to both Vietminh and French attacks. In essence, Ho and the French "agreed to disagree" on the questions of whether, how and when Cochin-China should become part of Ho's republic.

"I have just signed my death warrant," Ho sighed to Moutet. When he reached his hotel he found that the red carpet in front of his suite had disappeared completely.

The *modus vivendi* was "better than nothing," Ho told the French press. He knew that his comrades in Hanoi would consider his mission a failure, especially since that same year India, Indonesia, Burma, and the Philippines were winning their freedom from colonialism. Ho returned home deeply troubled, but determined to convince his people that the slow course toward bloodless revolution was better than civil war.

He was heartened by a tumultuous welcome in Haiphong harbor. By way of emphasizing the revolutionary implications of his pact with the French, he called upon the crowds to sing France's revolutionary national anthem, the "Marseillaise."

But the personal affection of the Vietnamese for their Uncle Ho did not save him from biting criticism in the Hanoi cabinet. Pro-Chinese leaders insisted that the *modus vivendi* was nothing less than a sell-out. "When a man remains in foreign countries for a long while," one said acidly, "he becomes their slave." A government announcement that Ho was ill led to speculation that he was under house arrest.

But on November 11, 1946, Ho was heard from when the French in Hanoi opened a customs house to supervise international imports entering Haiphong harbor. Shocked, Ho protested to the French prime minister that this act violated the *modus vivendi*. Bidault replied that the customs house was essential to stop illegal importation of arms and ammunition by the Vietminh. On November 20 a Chinese junk suspected as a gun-runner was stopped in Haiphong harbor by a French cutter which insisted upon searching it.

Vietminh troops at the port protested hotly. The argument led to a blazing gun battle. Colonel Dèbes, the French commander, received orders from Saigon to drive all Vietminh forces out of Haiphong and occupy the city.

"The time has come," General Valluy, acting high commissioner for Cochin-China, wired Dèbes, "to give a harsh lesson to those who have treacherously attacked us. By every means at your disposal, you must take control of Haiphong and bring the government and the Vietnamese army to repentance!"

Dèbes launched a full-scale attack on Haiphong with naval artillery support. Six thousand Vietnamese were killed in the bombardment. Shock waves convulsed the country.

Ho, ill with fever, called in French correspondents.

"This war is something we wish to avoid at all costs," he told them sadly. "We long passionately for independence, even if only within the French Union. War doesn't pay. But we cannot allow such slaughter as the price of freedom."

Giap, infuriated, wanted to signal an all-out attack on the French. The colonial generals, he told Ho, would never live up to any agreement until they were taught respect for the Vietminh power to enforce it. Ho persuaded him to give French public opinion a chance to shackle the Saigon military, but yielded to Giap's demands that they deploy their forces secretly in case war became necessary.

Disguised as peasants, Vietminh shock troops unobtrusively surrounded every French garrison in the country. Dynamite charges were concealed in the electric plants.

Meanwhile, Ho's friends in Paris provoked public indignation over the massacre in Haiphong. Bidault's government could not muster a vote of confidence, and fell. On December 12 the chamber of deputies called upon Leon Blum to form a new government. Blum at once dispatched Moutet to Hanoi to stop the French military from provoking a war.

But it was too late. Skirmishes between the Vietminh and French paratroops had broken out on the streets of Hanoi. On December 19, General Morlière, commander of the French garrison in Hanoi, ordered his troops to battle readiness. Then he demanded that Giap disband all Vietminh units in the city. This arrogant disregard for the independence and autonomy of their republic infuriated the Vietnamese.

With heavy heart Ho gave Giap his consent to war.

As the moon rose, electric plants in French garrisons suddenly blew up all over the country. In the confusion and darkness, Vietminh forces struck hard.

Calling upon his people for a "national war of resistance," Ho said bitterly, "In search of peace, we made concessions. But the more concessions we made, the more advantage was taken of us by French colonialists determined to invade our country once again. No more! We will sacrifice all before giving up our country. We shall never be enslaved!"

He urged Vietnamese to fight the French with whatever weapons they had—rifles, swords, spades, hoes or sticks. Appealing to the French people to curb their military, he also pleaded with the American people to come to the aid of the besieged Vietnamese. No longer a lamb of peace, Ho was now a tiger of war. A few months earlier he had told American correspondent David Schoenbrun that the French would be wise to think twice about provoking a war in Vietnam.

"If ever the tiger pauses, the elephant will impale him on his mighty tusks," he acknowledged, but added grimly, "The tiger will not pause, however, and the elephant will die of exhaustion and loss of blood!"

Even now, however, he could not give up hope that his friends in Paris could somehow bring about a reconciliation. He sent eight appeals for new negotiations.

"You are not to blame for this policy of force and reconquest," he wrote Sainteny on January 24, 1947. "Despite what has happened, you and I are still friends. And I can assure you that our two peoples are still friends, too. We have already had enough death and destruction! What are we to do now, you and I? France has only to recognize the independence and unity of Vietnam, and at once hostilities will cease, peace and trust will return."

Ho's appeals went unheeded in Paris. Ill health forced Blum's resignation early in January. When Communist ministers in the cabinet of his successor, Paul Ramadier, demanded a settlement with Ho, he dismissed them. One reason was France's eagerness for American Marshall Plan aid to anti-Communist countries. Another was the warning of De Gaulle, a growing force in French politics, that any premier responsible for the loss of a colonial territory would be compelled to stand trial for treason when De Gaulle came to power.

President Truman, pursuing a cold war to contain Soviet expansionism, turned a deaf ear to Ho's appeal for recognition. France was far more important to his new foreign policy than distant little Vietnam. The colonial French, moreover, were accusing Giap's forces of having committed dreadful atrocities against them in Hanoi.

"Four-fifths of the stories or reports of awful atrocities inflicted by the Vietnamese on our compatriots in Hanoi, December 19, 1946," later acknowledged Professor Paul Mus, political adviser to the new French high commissioner, "are either made up or in error." But they served to

alienate Western sympathy for Ho's government, and were
used by the French to justify violating their agreement with
him.

Ho realized that the meagerly-armed Vietminh could not
stand up to the military superiority of the French forces in
open combat. He urged Giap to withdraw their troops from
all cities to guerrilla strongholds in the countryside. This
retreat would not only spare the cities and occupants from
devastation, but would also siphon the French into fixed
positions from which they could be clawed.

Giap agreed with this strategy. Patriots before them had
also fled from the cities to the jungles and rice paddies,
fighting from the midst of the peasantry until the invaders
were finally driven out. Let the French have the cities,
bridges, industries, ports. Ho would have the most powerful
Vietnamese resource of all—the people.

In May 1947 French High Commissioner Emile Bolleart
sent Paul Mus on a secret mission to Ho. Walking north
from Hanoi through Vietminh lines, Mus was taken to meet
Ho at a hut in a mountain village. He had been sent, he told
Ho, to urge the Vietminh to call off the war. Ho asked him
what concessions France was prepared to make to indicate
recognition of the republic's independence and equality.

Mus admitted that he had been authorized only to offer
Ho back his seat in the French Union. After ordering the
Vietminh to lay down their arms, Ho would then be free to
appeal for a redress of Vietnamese grievances.

"Lay down our arms, Monsieur le professeur?" Ho replied incredulously. "But you know us better than that. My
only weapon is anger. I won't disarm my people until I trust
you. If I were to accept this demand for unconditional surrender, I would be a coward. The French Union is pre-

sumably an assemblage of free men, without any place in it for cowards."

He rose. "Would *you* accept such terms in *my* place?"

Mus, an honest man, had to admit that he would not. They shook hands gravely, and Ho walked back into the jungle to carry on seven more years of war against the French.

Years later Mus, who considered Ho "above genius, the greatest man I ever met," declared, "I have no reason, as a Frenchman, to like Ho for what has happened between our two countries, but I still like him. I am not afraid to say so. I like him for his strong mind. Although he is a great actor —one cannot afford to be naive with him—he does not go back on his word. He believes in the truth as he sees it, but he is a Marxist, and that is where we part company."

Mus felt that the French violation of the *modus vivendi* had been a blunder of the worst order: "We thought we could crush him if it came to war. We did not appreciate how hard he could fight. But we must not forget that he really wanted an agreement with France, because it would have served his interests. He was truly disappointed."

Ho infused his people with the need for patience to wear away the French presence in their country. He advocated that each Vietnamese sabotage the French any way he could.

"A pick stroke into the roads," he suggested, "has the value of a bullet shot by our soldiers at the enemy."

Sleeping in a crude hut near his soldiers, he directed the war from cave headquarters in which he typed troop orders, messages to the Vietminh political cadre, and war regulations that he himself obeyed like any peasant.

His directives were full of suggestions for assuring popular support: "Don't damage villagers' gardens and crops, houses and furniture. . . . Don't take live fowl into people's homes. . . . Tell bright stories (but don't give away national defense secrets). . . . Teach the alphabet and modern methods of hygiene." He reminded the guerrilla forces, "The palace of any victory is built upon the whole people."

Wearing a simple brown cotton tunic, covered by a torn lumber jacket in cold weather, Ho often ran with peasants to hide in the fields from French bombers. During quiet spells he would play volleyball with his aides, always diplomatically passing the ball to teammates to give them the glory of scoring winning shots.

The war made Giap almost as important a figure as Ho himself. A brilliant military tactician, he had personal as well as patriotic reasons for fighting the French without quarter. During World War II his wife had been taken a political prisoner by the Vichy French, and she had died in jail in 1943.

While Ho patterned their overall strategy on the teachings of Marx and Lenin, Giap modelled their military tactics after those of Mao Tse-tung's Red Army, which was then dealing stunning blows to Chiang Kai-shek's Nationalists.

Millions of Americans knew of Ho's struggle only through the eyes of William Bullitt, who expounded Bao Dai's views in *Life* magazine. Ho's independence movement was simply "another finger to the hand that Stalin is closing around [Nationalist] China," Bullitt insisted. No deal with Ho could be trusted because his promises would be broken whenever Moscow wished. Bullitt thought it would be a splendid idea if the French brought back Bao Dai as head of a "nationalist" regime that would "eliminate the Communists."

Bullitt's charges produced a flood of wires to Ho from foreign correspondents. Ho denied that his government was or ever could be a Russian satellite, and vowed a policy of Swiss-like neutrality for his republic. Asked if he would accept artillery and heavy mortars from the Chinese Red Army, he replied ironically, "What friendly advice would you give us in that case?"

The French, sensing that the Bullitt article was a semi-official statement of American policy, quickly took their cue. They prepared to set up Bao Dai, the one-time Japanese puppet, as Vietnamese head of state.

Leaving military strategy more and more in Giap's hands, Ho concentrated on the political aspects of their struggle. Hoping for Soviet aid, he sought to stay in the good graces of the Comintern, which after the war had become the Cominform. Moscow was furious at Tito of Yugoslavia for defying Stalin, and wanted leading world Communists to denounce him as a "deserter from Marxist-Leninist doctrine."

Ho formally obliged, while privately admiring Tito as his own kind of Marxist patriot, one who put his own country's welfare before any ideology. Tito was too shrewd not to know Ho's true sentiments, and announced Yugoslav recognition for the Democratic Republic of Vietnam, hopeful that Ho would decide to join him in breaking with Moscow.

Ho carefully declared that he was glad to establish relations with "any government" that recognized his own.

Ho's independence was probably the reason why Stalin

waited five years before giving him similar recognition. It came hastily, however, when Mao's new government of Red China, having driven Chiang Kai-shek into exile on Formosa in December 1949, recognized Ho's republic one month later. Ho then asked Mao for, and was promised, some of the American military supplies captured from Chiang's forces.

The French, unable to crush the Vietminh and having serious difficulties at home, appealed to Washington for financial and military aid in continuing the war. They pointed out that the aid Ho had been promised by Mao proved that Red China intended to make all Southeast Asia Communist, and that only support of French colonialism in Vietnam could prevent it.

On February 1, 1950, Secretary of State Dean Acheson stated that recognition of Ho's government by the USSR and Red China "should remove any illusions as to the 'Nationalist' nature of Ho Chi Minh's aims and reveals Ho in his true colors as the mortal enemy of native independence in Indo-China."

India's Nehru, visiting Washington, told Acheson that he misunderstood the situation in Southeast Asia; that a policy of support for the puppet Bao Dai regime was doomed to fail, and that only Ho's government had popular support. But Acheson was committed to Truman's cold war policy.

"After some hesitation," he wrote later in his biography, "we in the Department recommended aid to France . . . in combatting Ho's insurgency. . . . The aid was to be limited to economic and military supplies, stopping short of our own military intervention. . . . While we may have tried to muddle through and were certainly not successful, I could not think then or later of a better course. One can suggest, perhaps, doing nothing."

One important reason for the American decision to intervene in Vietnam on the side of France was that Paris was an important member of the NATO alliance directed against the Soviet Union in Europe. France's demand for United States support in Vietnam implied diplomatic blackmail. If Washington refused to act as an ally to Paris in Southeast Asia, why should Paris remain an ally to Washington in Europe?

So Acheson and Truman took the first fateful step to commit American power in Vietnam—a step that would have disastrous consequences for the United States over the next quarter of a century.

On February 2 France enacted the Elysée Accords establishing the Associated States of Indo-China—Cochin-China, Annam and Tonkin—under its puppet emperor, Bao Dai. Washington promptly recognized this new colonial creation, whose foreign relations, armed forces, and finances remained firmly under French control. American aid began to flow to Bao Dai, who, said the State Department, was "making sincere efforts to unite all truly national elements within Vietnam."

If Ho had had any last lingering hope of American friendship and recognition, Washington's support of the Bao Dai regime ended it. Now he knew that he could look only to Red China and the Soviet Union for help, and would have to pay whatever price was demanded of him.

Early in March 1950 Leo Figuères, leader of the French Young Communists, visited Ho in his secret mountain headquarters. Figuères found Ho confident of eventual victory. The triumph of Chinese Communism, Ho pointed out, not only gave the Vietnamese a powerful ally, but also opened China's southern border to them, ending their state of siege in the mountains and their isolation from the outside world.

He told Figuères that he was willing to discuss an exchange of prisoners with the French, in order to get negotiations for peace talks started. But if the French persisted in seeking to crush the republic, Ho and all his people were ready to spend their whole lives fighting an endless, permanent revolutionary war.

When Ho's offer was reported to Paris, Maurice Thorez, head of the French Communist party, declared, "It is precisely because we are patriotic Frenchmen, workers fired with the spirit of internationalism, that we are campaigning against the foul war in Vietnam. It is precisely because we love France that we suffer and are ashamed to learn that Frenchmen have been guilty of crimes."

But the French government fought on, confident that with the Americans now paying eighty percent of the cost of the war in Vietnam, the defeat of Ho Chi Minh was inevitable.

Victory at Dienbienphu

WHEN THE KOREAN WAR broke out in June 1950, Washington viewed it as a struggle to contain Red Chinese expansionism. Ho's fight against French colonialism was considered a flank operation by Red China in that struggle. The Pentagon wanted southern Vietnam held as an American base in the circle of military power it was building around China.

Truman funnelled hundreds of millions of dollars' worth of arms and supplies to the French in Saigon. An American mission of thirty-five military advisers was dispatched to train and direct Bao Dai's troops. In six short years, Roosevelt's anti-colonial policy for Southeast Asia had been transformed into Truman's policy of supporting French colonialism.

But the new aid Ho received from Mao Tse-tung enabled Giap to launch a skillful campaign that cut off and captured an entire line of French forts along the Chinese border.

In 1951 the militants in Ho's cabinet pressed him to rees-

tablish the Indo-Chinese Communist party, making it clear
that the Vietnamese were no longer fighting just for independence, but now also for a Communist nation. Ho refused, but pacified them with a compromise. He created a
new Lao Dong (Workers) party that took its Marxism
from the old ICP, but its nationalism from the Vietminh.

Giap's masterly generalship began to tell in 1952. He
inflicted a series of humiliating defeats upon the French,
who were bewildered by his unpredictable guerrilla tactics.
American military observers reached the conclusion that
the only way to fight Giap was to follow Mao Tse-tung's
famous precept, just as Giap did: "The people are like the
water; we must swim among them like fish." A U.S. Special
Forces unit was set up to organize, train, direct and arm
native forces in an anti-Communist underground movement.

Stalin's death in 1953 stunned Ho along with the rest of
the world. Although by this time Ho had few illusions about
the Russian dictator, he permitted pro-Moscow aides in his
cabinet to wreathe a portrait of Stalin in their jungle hide-
out with flowers and illuminate it with candles, as two of
them played violins during a brief memorial ceremony.

Would a struggle for power break out now in the Kremlin, Ho worried, that would put the war in Indo-China low
on the list of Russian priorities? He was anxious to involve
the Soviet Union in his defense, in order to keep from being
dependent solely upon Peking. He also wondered what the
new American president, Dwight D. Eisenhower, who had
negotiated an armistice in Korea, would do about Vietnam.

He was dismayed when Eisenhower, on the advice of

Secretary of State John Foster Dulles, decided to increase
American aid, but to channel it directly to Bao Dai rather
than through Paris. Dulles hoped in this way to make Bao
Dai a more convincing figure as a national leader, and to
give Washington more control over Saigon's policies.

Ho closely studied the president's remarks made at a
governor's conference on August 4, 1953: "Now let us assume that we lost Indo-China. If Indo-China goes, several
things happen right away. The peninsula, the last little bit of
land hanging on down there, would be scarcely defensible.
The tin and tungsten that we so greatly value from that area
would cease coming, and all India would be outflanked."

Eisenhower added, "So when the United States votes
$400 million to help that war, we are not voting a giveaway
program. We are voting for the cheapest way that we can
prevent the occurrence of something that would be of a
most terrible significance to . . . our security, our power and
ability to get certain things we need from the riches of the
Indonesian territory and from Southeast Asia."

This thinking reflected the views of Dulles, who believed
that it was necessary to go to the brink of war with the
Soviet Union and Red China in order to make them respect
American power and spheres of influence. He was also convinced that all non-Christian nations—Buddhist, Moslem
and atheist—were misguided and untrustworthy.

Nehru called Dulles' foreign policy a "bigoted, almost
religious approach to world affairs." The Indian prime minister warned, "Religion . . . is not good mixed up with
politics." Dulles was outraged by Nehru's refusal to join his
international crusade against Communism.

Realizing that the Eisenhower administration was determined to give full support to the French effort to crush him, Ho set out for both Peking and Moscow late in 1953. He won agreement from the Kremlin to pay Red China for supplies of surplus arms no longer needed in North Korea.

From Moscow Ho denounced the "criminal activities on the part of the United States for spreading the war of aggression in Asia," and charged "American intervention" as responsible for sabotaging his peace negotiations with the French.

Ho and Giap decided that they had to defeat the French swiftly before massive new American aid poured into Saigon. But the Vietminh had an army only three-fifths the size of the French colonial forces, and French fire power was ten times greater. Ho suggested that they exploit the chief French weakness, an obligation to use the colonial army to protect all members of the French Union.

So Giap launched diversionary attacks against Laos and Cambodia. The French frantically rushed paratroops all over Indo-China in a futile effort to contain the guerrillas. Then Giap sprang his trap, sending the main Vietminh army against the weakened key French stronghold at Dienbienphu.

Giap's timing was perfect. Only a speedy and massive intervention by American forces could save Dienbienphu. If it fell, the whole French presence in Vietnam was doomed.

The dilemma was humiliating for a nation that had senselessly spent its treasure, manpower and prestige on a bloody colonial war it could not win. By violating the *modus vivendi* signed with Ho, in order to reimpose their old obsolete colonialism on the Vietnamese, the French government had also badly divided their own people over the war.

On March 20, 1954, the French chief of staff, General Paul Ely, appealed to President Eisenhower. If the Americans did not intervene quickly in great force, he warned, France would be compelled to negotiate a settlement with Ho that would establish the Vietminh, now committed to Communism, as the legal government of all Vietnam. And what would that mean to the fate of the rest of Southeast Asia?

The American Joint Chiefs of Staff argued among themselves. The chairman, Admiral Arthur Radford, proposed "Operation Vulture"—sending three hundred carrier-based fighter bombers and sixty heavy bombers from the Philippines to obliterate the Vietminh besieging Dienbienphu. Dulles approved, suggesting that atomic warheads might be used, but General Matthew Ridgeway was vehemently opposed to both plans.

"When the day comes for me to face my Maker and account for my actions," Ridgeway wrote later in his memoirs, "the thing I would be most humbly proud of was the fact that I fought against, and perhaps contributed to preventing the carrying out of some hairbrained tactical schemes. . . . To that list of tragic accidents that fortunately never happened I would add the Indochina intervention."

Vice President Richard M. Nixon was among the hawks who subscribed to Dulles' "domino theory," which he continued to believe in and act upon later as president. Ho studied a report of Nixon's "off-the-record" views expressed to the American Society of Newspaper Editors on April 16, 1954, as they were summarized by the *New York Times*:

> The United States as a leader of the free world cannot afford further retreat in Asia. It is hoped the United States will not have to send troops there, but if this government

cannot avoid this, the Administration must face up to the situation and dispatch forces. . . . It should be emphasized that if Indo-China went Communist, Red pressures would increase on Malaya, Thailand, Indonesia and other nations. . . . This country is the only nation politically strong enough at home to take a position that will save Asia.

But Eisenhower, a general who hated war, was reluctant to allow the United States to be dragged any further into a bloody colonial war that might end in American troops being bogged down in land fighting in Southeast Asia. The trap that the French had blundered into, he knew, could also become a military disaster for Americans.

The president declared that he could not "conceive of a greater tragedy for America than to get involved now in an all-out war in any of those regions." As he saw it, military victory would not be possible, in any event, simply because of the political situation. The Vietnamese people supported the Vietminh and regarded Ho as their greatest patriot, Communist or not, trusting him to free them from the French.

"The enemy had much popular sympathy," Eisenhower wrote later in his memoirs, *Mandate for Change*, "and many civilians aided them by providing both shelter and information." The French, he noted, lacked popular support. The troops of their puppet, Bao Dai, simply would not fight against "Uncle Ho."

So Eisenhower restrained the war hawks in his administration as well as in the Pentagon. He simply advised the French to extricate themselves from their predicament through a settlement with Ho at an international peace conference.

Giap, meanwhile, pushed ahead with the battle for Dienbienphu. The French defenses were mercilessly pounded by artillery fired from Giap's camouflaged dugouts in the hills surrounding the base. The French had hoped to cut off the Vietminh from their supply line by bombing roads and bridges behind them. But Ho kept Giap supplied by bicycle brigades of thousands of peasants, each carrying four hundred pounds of materiel along jungle paths hidden from the air.

The Vietminh, on the other hand, were able to keep the Dienbienphu airstrip under continuous shellfire, cutting off the French from their supply line to Saigon.

Giap kept moving his troops and artillery forward to new concealed positions. The desperate French defenders found themselves being strangled in a noose drawn tighter and tighter around them. Each night the sound of Vietminh trenches being dug grew closer and closer. On May 6 a new weapon tore into the base. Rockets blasted apart bunkers weakened by rain and blew ammunition dumps sky-high.

As dawn broke, Giap lay down a withering barrage of artillery fire. Waves of Vietminh raced behind it, overrunning the French positions. One French unit after another was surrounded and either surrendered or was wiped out.

The last French guns fell quiet at 5:30 P.M., May 7. Dienbienphu fell hours later, ending the gruelling fifty-five-day siege. Notified by the jubilant Giap, Ho was silent a moment, then told Dong quietly, "It is a great victory, but it is only a beginning." He knew that the struggle for a free and united Vietnam was by no means over.

The following day the French government, after a presence in Indo-China that had lasted over three hundred years, sued for the peace that meant their departure from

Southeast Asia. With the fall of Dienbienphu, the Vietminh controlled three-quarters of Vietnam. The overjoyed Vietnamese once more acclaimed Ho Chi Minh the savior of their nation.

Participating in a peace settlement at Geneva were the Vietminh, the French, the British, the Russians, the Chinese, and the Americans. Dulles, however, withdrew to show his disapproval of concessions to Ho's republic, leaving behind Under-Secretary of State Walter Bedell Smith to "observe."

Dong, heading the Vietminh delegation, pressed for immediate and total withdrawal of the French, with all of Vietnam united and independent under Hanoi. France and Britain balked. Dong angrily warned that the Vietminh now possessed the power to enforce its demands by swift capture of the southern quarter of the country still in French hands.

But to Dong's chagrin, he was not supported by Soviet Foreign Minister Vyacheslav Molotov or Chinese Premier Chou En-lai. Moscow pressed the Vietminh to make concessions to France because the Russians wanted the Western powers to make concessions in Europe. The Chinese wanted the Vietminh to moderate their demands because of a private agreement with Nehru that Indo-China should become independent, neutral buffer states between them.

Dong appealed to Ho, who reluctantly yielded to the pressure from his allies. Ho knew that militant factions of his cabinet would be furious with him for not maintaining a hard line with the defeated French. But it would be unrealistic to defy both Peking and Moscow and expect his republic to survive. With a sigh of resignation he ordered Dong to accommodate their allies and get the best terms they could.

The Geneva Accords were signed on July 20, 1954, by the Vietminh and the French, and approved by Britain, the Soviet Union, Cambodia, Laos and the French puppet regime in Saigon. The settlement ended the war and divided Vietnam in half at the Seventeenth Parallel, "temporarily." Countrywide elections were to be held in two years under an International Control Commission (ICC), and would determine a unified government for all Vietnam. Election preparations would begin in one year.

Pending the elections, the Vietminh agreed to withdraw its military forces to the northern zone, while the French forces were to retreat to the southern zone. Both sides agreed not to take reprisals against dissenters within their zones. Such persons were to be guaranteed their democratic liberties, and those who chose to leave one zone to live in the other were to be helped to emigrate.

The French were to remain the governing power in the southern zone through their puppet, ex-Emperor Bao Dai, until the elections. The northern zone would be governed by Ho Chi Minh as both president and premier of his republic.

Dulles, who had followed the Geneva negotiations from Paris, was pressed by the UN to announce American acceptance of the Accords. Issuing a guarded statement "noting" the Geneva agreement, he promised the UN that the United States, while refusing to accept any responsibility for the armistice, would "refrain from the threat or the use of force to disturb" the settlement. He added that Washington "would view any renewal of the aggression . . . with grave concern."

But Dulles had already determined to nullify the clause of the Geneva Accords specifying that "the military demarcation line is provisional, and should not in any way be interpreted as constituting a political or territorial boundary." He began to maneuver secretly to transform the temporary southern zone into a permanent and separate nation, the American client state of South Vietnam.

The French and British viewed the Geneva Accords simply as a face-saving delay for Paris in acknowledging Ho's victory. They did not question the fact that Ho and the Vietminh would easily sweep the elections, whether these were held at once or two years later as scheduled. But the French hoped to get some economic concessions from Ho in exchange for their cooperation in carrying out the Accords.

Reentering Hanoi with his victorious troops, Ho arrived in a captured French army truck. Smaller than his shabby clothes, his mandarin beard frizzled and his hair now whiter, the sixty-five-year-old leader embraced Dong and other delegates who had returned from Geneva. The Vietminh planned a gala public celebration in Ho's honor, but he persuaded them to call it off. How could they celebrate, he asked sadly, when so much of their country lay in ruins?

Greeting hundreds of guerrilla leaders gathered in a reception hall of the palace, he praised and thanked them.

"I'm an old guerrilla fighter, too, you know," he reminded them. His gentle humility, part genuine, part the performance of a skilled actor, endeared him to a whole new generation of young patriots. They saw "Uncle Ho" as the very model of the traditional Vietnamese village elder.

Hailed as the father of his country, he encouraged the

personal affection of his people by declaring, "I was never married. I never had time. But I have seventeen million children." He kissed babies enthusiastically and offered gallant, witty compliments to women that made them blush in delight. Veteran observers agreed that it would take a miracle for any rival to beat Uncle Ho at the polls.

Ho's cabinet was split between rival pro-Chinese and pro-Soviet ministers. A canny diplomat, Ho resisted the pressure from both sides and sought to use each Communist giant for his own purposes. "There is no doubt that while his heart is in Moscow," observed American diplomat Averell Harriman, "his stomach is in Peking." Cut off from the fertile rice fields of southern Vietnam, he needed Chinese rice to feed his people in the northern zone.

Ho carefully watched Washington's moves, suspicious of Dulles's intentions in Vietnam. The secretary of state had caused a statement to be issued from the White House on July 21: "The United States has not itself been a party to or bound by the decisions taken by the Geneva Conference. . . . The agreement contains features which we do not like, but a great deal depends on how they work in practice."

Dulles had been impressed by the success of Ramon Magsaysay in defeating the Communist Huk guerrillas in the Philippines. He called in Colonel Edward Lansdale, the CIA operative who had masterminded that operation, and ordered him to find a "Vietnamese Magsaysay." This native leader's job would be to hold southern Vietnam against the Vietminh when it came time for the French army to withdraw.

Central to Dulles's plan was sabotage of the elections scheduled for 1956 by the Geneva Accords.

"I have never talked or corresponded with a person knowledgeable in Indochinese affairs," Eisenhower admitted later in *Mandate for Change*, "who did not agree that had the elections been held as of the time of the fighting, possibly 80 per cent of the population would have voted for Ho Chi Minh."

Dulles was determined to see that they didn't get the chance. He had other plans for southern Vietnam.

America Gets Involved

COLONEL LANSDALE'S SEARCH for a "Vietnamese Magsay-say" narrowed down to a small, pudgy fifty-three-year-old Catholic politician, Ngo Dinh Diem. The conservative Diem had served as a minister in the colonial French government at Saigon, but had quit when his plea for reform was ignored.

His anti-Communist views had impressed a Michigan State University team secretly working for the CIA in southern Vietnam. This group had sent him to the United States in 1950 to win support as the American choice to replace Bao Dai. Diem had convinced influential Americans like Cardinal Spellman, Senator John F. Kennedy and Senator Mike Mansfield that he could lead a "third force" in Vietnam, holding a middle course between France's discredited colonialism and Ho's Communism.

When Colonel Lansdale arrived in Saigon just after the fall of Dienbienphu, he found southern Vietnam in utter military and political chaos. Consulting with Diem, Lansdale became convinced that only Diem, backed by Washington, could keep Bao Dai's Saigon regime from crumbling.

But Eisenhower was skeptical about Dulles's insistence that they pressure the French to foist Diem on Bao Dai as premier. It might be disastrous, the president pointed out, for the United States to put its prestige behind a Vietnamese who had at best the support of only the 10 percent of his countrymen who were Catholics, against the indisputable great popularity of Ho Chi Minh. But Dulles urged him to take the risk.

Diem's American supporters added their own pressure.

"If Geneva and what was agreed upon there means anything at all," Cardinal Spellman told an American Legion convention on August 31, 1954, "it means . . . Taps for the buried hopes of freedom in Southeast Asia! Taps for the newly betrayed millions of Indochinese who must now learn the awful facts of slavery from their eager Communist masters! . . . Do you peacefully coexist with men who would thus train the youth of their godless, Red world?"

Leo Cherne, an anti-Communist adviser to American corporations, cabled back his views from Saigon:

U.S. EMBASSY, STRONGLY SUPPORTING DIEM, VIEWS HIM AS KEY TO WHOLE SITUATION. POLITICAL AND FINANCIAL INSTABILITY . . . UNLESS VIETNAMESE GOVERNMENT CAN ORGANIZE IMPORTANT FORCES AND U.S. CONTINUES POURING IN SUBSTANTIAL HELP AND MONEY. . . . IF FREE ELECTIONS HELD TODAY ALL AGREE PRIVATELY COMMUNISTS WOULD WIN.

Eisenhower yielded, and Dulles arranged for Diem to become premier of Bao Dai's regime as a first step in replacing French with American influence in southern Vietnam.

On September 8, at Manila, Dulles then brought SEATO (Southeast Asia Treaty Organization) into being, "to promote the security of all free peoples . . . [against] Communist subversion" in Indo-China. SEATO pledged the U.S., England, France, Australia, New Zealand, the Philippines, Pakistan, Thailand, and South Vietnam as a "protocol state," to come to the aid of any member nation threatened by Communism.

Any attempt by Ho to unify Vietnam in 1956, in keeping with the provisions of the Geneva Accords, could now be countered by Diem's appeal to SEATO to "save South Vietnam from Communism," giving Dulles a legal pretext for sending in American forces to rescue Diem's regime from "subversion."

On New Year's Day, 1955, a five-hour anti-American demonstration took place in Hanoi, obviously staged by Ho's government. "We must be on guard," Ho told huge crowds, "against plans of the imperialistic Americans, who are planning to intervene in Indo-China, to incite their lackeys to sabotage the armistice and bring about a return of war."

There were many factions in southern Vietnam itself equally opposed to Diem. Lansdale warned American General J. Lawton Collins that they were planning a coup. When civil war broke out in Saigon in the spring of 1955, Collins saw to it that Diem was able to crush it in fifteen hours.

As the Geneva Accords required, Ho issued an order permitting all those who wished to leave the northern zone of Vietnam to go south. Washington had offered to pay a resettlement cost of ninety-eight dollars per refugee. Almost nine hundred thousand emigrated.

Half a million, reported the *Survey of International Affairs*, were Catholics, many of them frightened by their priests' warnings that the Americans planned to drop an atomic bomb on the Communist north. Some felt that they would be safer and better off under a Catholic premier than a Red president.

Non-Catholic émigrés included Vietnamese who feared reprisals for having fought with French native forces against the Vietminh, small landlords driven off their holdings by a new Hanoi collectivization program, and Vietnamese eager to benefit from the prosperity they knew that a huge influx of American money would bring to the southern zone.

Ho was quite content to have the refugees leave. The plan rid him of most opponents of his regime, leaving him with almost seventeen million largely loyal followers. Ho also expected Diem to show favoritism to the Catholic refugees, angering the 90 percent Buddhist population.

For the first two years of their resettlement, American aid provided the refugees with land, cleared it for them, provided tractors, training and seed, gave them food and materials for homes and schools. Diem used their villages as showplaces to display to American visitors as examples of his own efficient administration. But as Ho shrewdly foresaw, such benefits showered on Catholics from the north provoked deep resentment among Buddhist peasants of the south.

A young American naval doctor named Tom Dooley aided in the transfer of refugees to the south. Crediting all the anti-Vietminh stories they told him, he returned to America to write and lecture about the Vietnamese "patriots" who had fought on the side of the French, and the "demons of Communism" who were "holding the upper half of the country in their strangling grip." Widely disseminated, Dooley's views helped Diem get billions in aid from Congress.

A somewhat different view of Communist rule in Vietnam was provided for the small readership of *The New Yorker* in June 1955. After taking a trip through the Mekong Delta in the south, which was under Vietminh control, veteran American correspondent Joseph Alsop reported:

> I would like to be able to report—I had hoped to be able to report—that on that long, slow canal trip . . . I saw all the signs of misery and oppression. . . . But it was not so. At first it was difficult for me, as it is for any Westerner, to conceive of a Communist government's genuinely "serving the people." I could hardly imagine a Communist government that was also a popular government and almost a democratic government. But this is just the sort of government the palm-hut state actually was. . . . The Vietminh could not possibly have carried on the resistance for one year, let alone nine years, without the people's strong, united support.

The Vietminh of the delta, who later became Viet Cong, reflected Ho's own unique brand of Communism. U Thant of Burma, who spent two days in Hanoi with Ho, reported, "I found him, as a Communist, strikingly independent in his thinking—quite like Tito . . . politically perceptive and de-

voted to his people . . . anxious to secure Vietnam's neutrality, quite like Burma."

Many Vietminh in the delta and other regions of the
southern zone wanted to go north in the exchange of refugees, but Ho discouraged them. He did not want to weaken
his voting and guerrilla strength in the south. About one
hundred fifty thousand nevertheless went north, mostly in
fear of Diem's secret police.

"The degree of cooperation given by the parties of North
and South Vietnam has not been the same," reported the
ICC supervising the peace terms. "While the Commission
has experienced difficulties in North Vietnam, the major
part of its difficulties has arisen in South Vietnam." The
ICC noted that the Hanoi regime had been helpful to the
point of supplying food and money for refugees going
south.

Ho sought to abide by the provisions of the Geneva Accords because he was counting on the elections of 1956 to
unite an independent Vietnam under his presidency. Diem,
encouraged by the United States, was determined to sabotage the Geneva Accords, knowing that the required elections would mean his downfall and the end of any "South
Vietnam."

To increase the inadequate rice crop of the northern
zone, Truong Chinh, Ho's pro-Chinese minister of agricul-
ture, decided to emulate Mao Tse-tung's "Great Leap Forward." In the name of "agrarian reform," Chinh ordered all
"exploiting landlords" dispossessed, and their lands expro-
priated by peasant tenants to be run as collective farms.

In actuality, the "rich" landlords who were targets of
land seizure were often mere peasants themselves, little bet-

ter off than their tenants. The latter were authorized to arrest landlords who resisted and, if necessary, to kill them. Chinh thus forced the peasants to share the guilt in this brutal method of setting up communes quickly, just as Mao Tse-tung had done in the rural areas of Red China.

Over six thousand farmers in Nghé An province finally rebelled in November 1956. When Chinh ordered the army to suppress their revolt mercilessly, he became the most hated man in northern Vietnam. Ho felt compelled to act.

Although he knew that it would anger Red China, he fired Chinh as secretary-general of the Lao Dong party. His cabinet insisted that he assume the portfolio himself to restore popular confidence in the Hanoi government.

The pro-Russian Giap was given the task of publicly expiating the Lao Dong party's sins. He denounced Chinh for having "executed too many people" and for having "resorted to terror, which became too widespread." He estimated that a third of the people condemned as "feudalists" had been wrongfully arrested and convicted.

But these admissions, like Ho's firing of Chinh, came two years after the fact. Ho could not have been ignorant of what was going on. His support of Chinh had to be assumed until the peasant revolt in Ho's own native Nghé An province flashed a danger signal. Only then was Chinh sacrificed as a scapegoat. There was unquestionably steel behind the gentle manners of soft-spoken Uncle Ho, who obviously still believed, as a dedicated, lifelong revolutionary, that noble ends justified ignoble means.

The French, Washington and the Diem regime were not slow in making the most of the Truong Chinh affair.

"They murdered more than 50,000 people," accused Vice President Nixon, "and hundreds of thousands more died in slave labor camps." He called it "a blood bath." The ICC investigated, but found no evidence of reprisal killings on a scale that could be called a massacre, nor any trace of mass deaths in slave labor camps.

The Commission, in fact, had received far more complaints of repressive measures being enacted under Diem. He had established a secret police force, the Vietnamese Bureau of Investigation (VBI), which spread fear by fingerprinting the population. Dissenters, political rivals and those simply suspected of disloyalty were arrested and sent to camps where torture formed a part of their "re-education." Conservative American estimates, early in 1956, put the number of political prisoners in Diem's concentration camps at twenty thousand.

Merchants, landlords and profiteers who had prospered under French colonial rule continued to flourish under Diem. Every officer in his army over the rank of major, with only two exceptions, had fought for the French. Diem permitted army and government officials to feather their nests with American funds and to sell U.S. supplies on the black market. Corruption was the order of the day in Saigon.

Most southern rice lands were held by absentee landlords, who collected usurious rents from poor tenants through Diem's local province and district chiefs. One percent of landlords owned almost half the land. Diem's American advisers insisted that he had to institute a land reform program if the peasants were to be wooed away from their devotion to Ho. But Diem knew that any attempt at real land reform would bring about his overthrow by the land-lord class. So he "liberated" land for peasants in a way that compelled them to continue paying the same rent to the same landlords.

One cynical American correspondent observed that Diem "believed in democracy, but felt compelled to ration it." Not only did Diem crush all political opposition ruthlessly, but he also ordered his police to shoot anyone even suspected of being a Viet Cong, as southern Vietminh were now known. He offered prizes for Vietnamese who denounced family or friends.

For the first five years of his regime, Diem arrested or murdered one hundred fifty thousand political opponents, liquidating tens of thousands of others who simply wanted the Geneva Accords implemented. Such police state tactics were themselves violations of the Accords, but Diem, unlike Ho, refused to allow the ICC to investigate. American officials in Saigon nevertheless praised Diem for having achieved order and stability.

The CIA, which had trained Diem's secret police, palace guard, and army officers, sought to persuade the peasantry to trust Saigon. Colonel Lansdale sent native "Civic Action" teams around the southern countryside to show propaganda films extolling Diem. This "pacification" program backfired because the only Vietnamese willing to join the teams were refugees from the north. Their different dialect, different religion and obvious American backing provoked resentment in the villages they toured for the CIA.

On March 9, 1955, Eisenhower had written a letter to Diem committing the United States to assist his regime "in developing and maintaining a strong, viable state." This

letter was backed by a billion dollars in military and economic aid between 1955 and 1960.

In the summer of 1955, as preparations for the national
elections of 1956 were scheduled to begin, Diem organized
demonstrations against the Geneva Accords. The day of
their signing, he cried, was "a national day of shame!" His
agents burned the hotel lodging the ICC commissioners in
Saigon.

On August 9 Diem wrote Ho that he would not allow the
elections to be held in the south. "We have not signed the
Geneva Accords," Diem insisted. "We are not bound in any
way by those agreements." Ho was outraged.

The accords, signed by the French and the Vietminh, had
been guaranteed by all nations at the international conference at Geneva except the United States. Yet even Washington had pledged not to interfere with their implementa-
tion.

On August 20 Dulles officially supported Diem's violation of the accords. He declared that conditions did not
exist for a truly free election, despite guarantees of international supervision by the ICC, whose commissioners represented Canada, India and Poland. The U.S. Lawyers
Committee on American Policy Toward Vietnam pointed
out that Dulles' support of the Diem regime as an independent nation was illegal: "Under the Geneva Accords of
1954, South Vietnam is merely a temporary zone not even
qualifying politically as a state."

The militants in Hanoi angrily reproached Ho for having
allowed himself to be cheated of Vietnamese unification at
the conference table, by pledges of elections which the
United States had never intended to allow. There was only

one course left open to them now, they insisted. The Vietminh themselves had to carry out the intent of the Geneva Accords, unifying the country by forcibly throwing out the illegal Saigon regime.

But Ho, deeply troubled, was worried over how far the United States meant to go in keeping its puppet in power. He knew he could win a civil war against Diem easily, because Diem had no popular support. But how could the Vietminh prevail if the United States decided to send an army, its Pacific fleet and giant air armada against them?

Meanwhile in the south a struggle for power was growing between Bao Dai and Diem. On October 18, acting on French advice, Bao Dai fired Diem as premier. Coached by Lansdale, Diem refused to resign and ordered a "referendum" in South Vietnam, asking the people to choose between Bao Dai, who had been discredited as a tool of the French, and himself. No one else was allowed on the ballot.

Diem's brother-in-law Ngo Dinh Nhu, chief of the secret police, censored the press and mobilized bloc votes of Catholics and the army. Anti-Diem voters were intimidated from entering the polls. Even so, Diem received less than a third of the votes cast. Nhu nevertheless declared him "elected by a plurality of 98 per cent." Three days later Diem proclaimed his own Republic of Vietnam.

Foreign correspondents in Saigon scoffed at Diem's "election," especially after Dulles's claim that the ICC could not guarantee free national elections. The State Department was silent on the legitimacy of its puppet state, except in later references to Diem's regime as "an elected government."

To provide the new regime with at least a semblance of democracy, Lansdale urged Diem and Nhu to permit some non-Communist opposition parties to function, and to stop persecuting political opponents. Diem and Nhu flatly refused. Angered, Lansdale flew to Washington to insist that Diem be compelled to abandon his dictatorship.

To Landsdale's chagrin, he learned that the National Security Council had decided that Diem had to be supported without reservation, as the only hope of preventing a Communist takeover. Nhu's secret police were to be expanded, trained, and directed by the CIA into a paramilitary unit. Because the Geneva Accords prohibited any military buildup by either side, the United States needed a "cover" to do this.

Vice President Nixon phoned John Hannah, president of Michigan State University, and arranged for the university's team of professors in Saigon to serve as a front for Washington. The Michigan State team organized and armed a "Civil Guard" of 40,000 militia to "pacify" the countryside.

They overthrew peasant-elected village councils created by the Vietminh, replacing these with province and district chiefs appointed by Saigon. All peasants were fingerprinted and issued identity cards. Villages offering resistance to the Civil Guard were shelled by artillery. Afterwards those who had not fled were arrested. Landlords who had been driven out by the Vietminh returned with the Civil Guard to reclaim their lands, collecting back taxes and rents in full.

Millions of South Vietnamese who had not been Communists were driven by Diem's "pacification" program into the rapidly swelling ranks of Viet Cong guerrillas. Most of this opposition was centered in the Mekong Delta, too distant for any support from Ho in the north.

"The insurrection existed before the Communists decided to take part, and they were simply forced to join in," observed French historian Philippe Devillers. "And even among the Communists the initiative did not originate in Hanoi, but from the grassroots, where the people were literally driven to take up arms in self-defense."

When some professors with the Michigan State team sought to bring about social and political reforms in the Diem regime, their efforts were contemptuously ignored. Many returned home frustrated, uneasy about the role they had played in saddling the people in the southern half of Vietnam with a corrupt and brutal dictatorship.

9

Between Russian Bear
and Chinese Dragon

IN HANOI, MEANWHILE, Ho was seeking to build North Vietnam into a model Communist state, not only to give his people a better life, but also to set an example to all of Southeast Asia. Beginning in 1956 he mounted a crash school program to wipe out illiteracy and give every child at least seven years in primary school and three in high school.

Jean Sainteny turned up in Hanoi as the French delegate-general. He found the sixty-six-year-old Asian leader "his old self, in good health, hardly a day older." Seated beside Ho at diplomatic dinners, Sainteny was shown preference over other guests. Ho also invited him to private dinners, hoping to work out a new understanding with his old enemy France.

"We have knocked each other about a good deal," Ho told Sainteny with a little smile. "Now we must work together on a fifty-fifty basis." He offered the French trade concessions in exchange for economic aid and help in developing heavy industry. Such French assistance would permit Ho to be less dependent on both Moscow and Peking.

But Paris was reluctant, fearful that Diem would take reprisals against French plantations and other commercial enterprises in South Vietnam. Paris was also anxious not to offend Washington, which had made clear its intention to oppose Ho's regime at all costs. Ho, disappointed, quarreled with Sainteny, who departed for Paris.

In February 1956 Ho found himself facing a new dilemma. At the Twentieth Soviet Congress in Moscow, Communist party chief Nikita Khrushchev repudiated Stalinism and proclaimed a new policy of peaceful coexistence with the West. Ho was startled. Did this mean Soviet assent to what he now regarded as American colonialism in Vietnam?

The new Soviet policy was also coolly received by Red China, which felt directly threatened by its encirclement with American military bases and treaties. Mao Tse-tung, seeking to woo Ho away from Moscow, began helping him build the heavy industry Ho wanted, and supplied a tenth of the rice he needed to feed his people.

Ho left Hanoi on a world trip to win support for his struggle against the Americans. Out of long habit as a revolutionary, he traveled light, his only baggage a portable typewriter and a change of cotton tunic, scarf and sandals cut from old tires. To demonstrate his independence of the Kremlin he visited neutral India, where he was warmly embraced by Nehru, and Poland, which had just defied Moscow by setting up a more independent government. Premier Wladyslaw Gomulka received Ho as a senior Communist statesman.

In Moscow Ho attended the November celebration of the Russian Revolution, and sought to commit the Kremlin to an aid program that would balance Red China's. But Khrushchev was reluctant to antagonize Washington. In Hanoi, where the pro-Chinese Truong Chinh had been allowed to return to Ho's cabinet as a concession to Peking for its aid, Chinh announced that further American aid to Saigon would be countered by more aid to Hanoi from Red China.

Significantly, nothing was said of Soviet aid.

In May 1957 Ho's enemy Diem, having crushed the Buddhist sects and politicians who opposed him, flew to the United States on the president's personal plane, the *Columbine*. At official functions arranged by the State Department, he was acclaimed as the "courageous statesman" who had "saved Vietnam from Communism." Mayor Robert Wagner welcomed him to New York City as a Southeast Asian leader "to whom freedom is the very breath of life itself."

Life magazine joined in the chorus of praise, but admitted, "Behind a facade of photographs, flags and slogans there is a grim structure of decrees, 're-education centers,' secret police. . . . The whole machinery of security has been used to discourage active opposition of any kind."

Diem was candid about who deserved the credit.

"Your aid enables us to hold this crucial spot," he told American notables at a dinner in his honor, "and to hold it at less expense to you and at less danger to the world than you could have done it yourself."

In 1959 the Viet Cong appealed to the Communists in North Vietnam to help their struggle to overthrow Diem.

Many VC leaders were annoyed at Ho's reluctance to violate the Geneva Accords. Weren't both Diem and the Americans doing it? Did Uncle Ho want the Vietnamese people to be one people, united and independent, or didn't he?

The militants in Ho's cabinet put pressure on him to agree. For five years, they pointed out, the North had abided by the accords, even after Diem and the Americans had refused to permit the scheduled elections. And what had the Soviet Union done to stop the United States from arming Diem? Nothing! Yet Moscow expected Ho to go along with their "peaceful co-existence" policy because it benefited the Soviet Union. How did that benefit Vietnam?

Ho was forced to agree to the appointment of militant Le Duan as head of the Lao Dong party. Le Duan began secretly to send a cadre of southern Communists, who had come north after the accords, back into South Vietnam to work secretly with the Viet Cong. The anti-Diem forces began stepping up their political and military subversion. The Saigon regime was thrown into turmoil by a wave of arson, sabotage, attacks on Civil Guard posts, and assassinations of Diem's village chiefs.

The United States poured in hundreds of millions of dollars in cash and goods for "pacification" of the peasantry in South Vietnam. Little of this aid reached the people because Diem's corrupt officials siphoned most of it off. In a desperate effort to stop the corruption, Washington increased its civilian personnel in Saigon from two thousand to over thirty thousand between 1960 and 1965. This new bureaucracy failed to make "pacification" work, while Saigon's merchants and Diem's officials continued to grow rich on the stolen American goods which they sold to the black market.

Upon returning from Vietnam, one disillusioned Michigan State University economist admitted, "After six years of large-scale American aid, Vietnam is becoming a permanent mendicant. Certainly, if aid were eliminated tomorrow, there would be an unpaid army and unfed civilians. American aid has built a castle on sand."

Washington, anxious to diminish Communist influence in the countryside, compelled Diem to agree to land reform. But under the program he put into effect, landlords were allowed to return to regions they had fled years before, collect rents they hadn't collected for years, and get paid for land confiscated eight years earlier by the Vietminh, who had given it to the peasant tenants. Diem's "land reform" was fiercely resented by the peasants, especially in the Mekong Delta. Popular support for the Viet Cong soared.

Frustrated, early in 1959 Washington paid for a new "Agroville" program that compelled peasants in Viet Cong territory to resettle in new Government-controlled villages they were forced to build themselves. This program, too, was a failure. Villagers sought the protection of the Viet Cong against ARVN (Saigon army) forces that sought to drag them from their homes, villages and rice fields.

By that summer the American people were beginning to become aware of the appalling waste, corruption and mismanagement in the U.S. aid program in South Vietnam. American correspondents also revealed the widespread hatred for the Diem regime, which was in danger of crumbling.

Diem, worried that American public opinion might force

Washington to cut off the massive aid he depended upon, now began raising a new alarm. South Vietnam, he charged, was being overrun by "Communist terrorists from the North."

In actuality a small, weakly armed cadre of Communists, mostly born in the South, were being infiltrated back to their home provinces by Le Duan. By raising the spectre of a huge Red invasion, Diem hoped to divert American attention from the corruption and unpopularity of his regime.

It was an old trick and it worked. Washington intensified American military involvement to prop up Diem.

Ho, meanwhile, found himself trapped in a new political crisis. The gap between Red China and the Soviet Union had widened into angry hostility. Most Communist nations were being pressured to choose between the two camps. Ho felt that he could not afford to make that choice. He needed the support of both Communist giants against the increasing military intervention of the United States in Vietnam.

Visiting Peking in 1959 for the tenth anniversary of the Chinese Revolution, Ho was careful to stand between Mao Tse-tung and chief Soviet delegate Mikhail Suslov. In private negotiations, he managed to win pledges of additional arms and aid from both Peking and Moscow, but adroitly declined their offers to send "volunteer" troops or military advisers. Ho knew that if either the Russian bear or the Chinese dragon were allowed to thrust a foot inside Hanoi's door, that door would gradually be forced open until North Vietnam lost its independence and became a captive nation.

At the third congress of the Lao Dong in September 1960, Ho was once more unanimously elected president of

North Vietnam, and given a mandate to reunify North and South Vietnam as one nation, Communist but independent. He relinquished his powers as head of the Lao Dong party to Le Duan, but a new national constitution gave him almost unlimited powers as head of state.

Soviet and Red Chinese observers at the congress watched carefully for hints as to which nation was favored. Peking was encouraged by the fact that the pro-Soviet Giap seemed to be in eclipse as a result of the maneuvering of Truong Chinh, who had never forgiven Giap for attacking him after the land reform fiasco. But Moscow was encouraged by the downgrading of General Nguyen Chi Thanh, a rival of Giap's and a staunch supporter of Red China.

If one development canceled the other, Ho's subtle political maneuvers were directed toward that end. The survival of his country, he felt, depended upon his ability to keep it balanced halfway between both Communist camps. Despite his private preference for Moscow, and bitter recollections of Chinese prisons, he could not do without Peking's rice.

In November, when a row broke out between China and Russia over Albania's pro-Chinese actions, Ho offered his services as an impartial Communist peacemaker. They were accepted, and he flew to Moscow to help avoid the open split that would put him in the awkward position of having to choose one bastion of support and lose the other.

By April 1960 Diem's regime was so widely detested that eighteen conservative South Vietnamese nobles, including some former ministers, challenged his rule in a public petition. They protested that the prisons were overflowing with political prisoners, and that Diem's bureaucracy was corrupt and inefficient. If he refused to reform his regime, they

predicted "soaring waves of hatred and resentment of a terribly suffering people standing up to break their chains."
 But Diem was persuaded to stand firm by Madame Nhu, his fanatical sister, and her husband, Ngo Dinh Nhu. In November 1960, a group of discontented young army officers rose in revolt. They were joined by thousands of civilians in a march on Diem's palace. Forces loyal to Diem crushed the uprising, killing four hundred rebels.

It was now no longer possible for Diem's apologists in the United States to acclaim him as an "apostle of freedom" who had singlehandedly held back the tide of Communism in Southeast Asia. *Time* magazine admitted, "Pleading the Communist threat, Diem has ruled with rigged elections, a muzzled press, and political re-education camps that now hold 30,000." Time was running out for the dictator.

A month after the revolt a broad united front of anti-Diem opposition was formed secretly in South Vietnam. The new National Liberation Front (NLF) was a coalition of Viet Cong, Buddhist groups, conservatives, liberals, young army officers and non-Communist peasant leaders.

Mostly native South Vietnamese, they angrily denied Diem's charges that they were infiltrators from the North. It was Diem, they pointed out, who depended upon northern immigrants—the refugees—for what little support he had. Admittedly, Communist influence in the NLF was strong, but the Communists were South Vietnamese, and were also committed to cooperating in a broad-based popular government for Saigon. The question of unifying the two Vietnams would be for such a coalition regime to decide.

The Viet Cong, now recognized as the guerrilla army of

the NLF, also included non-Communist elements. Many guerrillas were part-time soldiers who farmed when not needed for fighting and picked up rifles under attack. Some were armed with weapons made in secret village workshops. Most Viet Cong fought with French and American arms stolen or captured from Diem's troops, who had little appetite for standing up to the guerrillas.

In January 1961, Lansdale, now a major general, was sent back to Vietnam by president-elect John F. Kennedy to assess the situation. Lansdale found the Diem regime intensely unpopular, its hold on power precarious. "The Vietnamese need a cause," Lansdale reported, "and we have not supplied it."

Sterling Cottrel, a State Department official, argued that Washington had no alternative but to continue to support an "Oriental dictator" like Diem, although Diem could not claim control of even a third of South Vietnam, despite all the massive aid the United States had poured into Saigon.

In an attempt to bolster Diem's shaky regime, Kennedy sent Vice President Lyndon B. Johnson to Saigon in May 1961. Johnson made eulogistic speeches comparing Diem to George Washington, Andrew Jackson, Woodrow Wilson, Franklin D. Roosevelt and Winston Churchill. But upon his return, Johnson privately told Kennedy that the United States faced an awkward choice; it could admit that its support of Diem and Saigon had been a bad mistake, and get out of Vietnam, or commit major American forces to holding Southeast Asia.

Kennedy, already humiliated by his unsuccessful Bay of Pigs invasion of Castro's Cuba, decided he could not afford a fresh military disaster in Vietnam. He ordered an intensification of American aid for Diem. The United States was soon spending $1.5 million a day to rescue Diem's regime.

On the advice of Professor Eugene Staley of Stanford University, the discredited Agroville program was revived in a new version called "Strategic Hamlets." Peasants were taken off the land their families had lived on for generations, and placed in government compounds to "protect" them from the Viet Cong. The real reason was to deny the VC their help and extend Diem's control of the countryside.

Lansdale protested to Washington, branding the Strategic Hamlets plan a police state use of concentration camps and genocide. "You don't put the people you're fighting for in a cage!" he pointed out sardonically.

The new millions in aid for the Strategic Hamlets program further enriched Chief and Madame Nhu, started Diem's generals quarreling over their share of the loot, and infuriated the peasantry. Volunteers for the Viet Cong doubled in one year.

By October Washington could no longer avoid recognizing that only swift and drastic reforms could prevent a new revolutionary explosion in South Vietnam. Kennedy sped a mission to Saigon, headed by his military adviser, General Maxwell Taylor. Taylor told Diem that he was recommending to the president sweeping land reforms, restoration of freedom of speech, increased democracy, release of political prisoners and replacement of Diem's corrupt generals by young officers.

Diem was furious. His controlled press ran angry blasts

against the United States. Washington was accused of interfering with Saigon's internal affairs, seeking "profits under the exploitation policy of capitalist imperialism." Diem's lobbyists in Washington echoed his indignation.

Kennedy felt compelled to water down the demands for political reforms Taylor deemed essential, and instead increased military and economic support for Diem. Secret decisions were made. The ARVN army was to be increased from one hundred fifty thousand to two hundred fifty thousand, another violation of the Geneva Accords. To train, equip and direct the ARVN as an effective fighting force, a cadre of fifteen thousand American "military advisers" would be sent.

Undersecretary of State George Ball opposed this move, warning that it might eventually suck over three hundred thousand American troops into a land war in Southeast Asia. General Lauris Norstad agreed: "The moment the first American arrives in Vietnam to shoot or be shot at, there's no way left open to us but escalation."

But the Pentagon, Secretary of Defense Robert McNamara, and Secretary of State Dean Rusk believed the risk worth taking. *New York Times* editor James Reston later revealed why Kennedy decided to agree. The president, returning from a meeting with Khrushchev in Vienna, had told Reston that the Soviet premier had decided that "anybody stupid enough to get involved in [the Bay of Pigs invasion] was immature, and anybody who didn't see it through was timid and, therefore, could be bullied."

To change Khrushchev's dangerous estimate of him, Reston explained, Kennedy had violated his promise not to involve America in an Asian war, and had sent the first thousands of "military advisers" to crush the civil war erupting in South Vietnam.

When Ho charged that American forces were fighting beside the ARVN, the Pentagon denied it. American correspondents reported that they were leading units in combat, however, as well as flying helicopters and planes. The Pentagon then insisted that the Americans were with the ARVN forces only in "an advisory and training capacity," firing weapons only in self-defense. That year, 1961, the first American soldier died in combat in South Vietnam.

Ho was able to get a small supply of arms and men to the Viet Cong over the "Ho Chi Minh Trail" that wound through the jungles on the Laotian and Cambodian side of the west Vietnam border. CIA Special Forces trained Vietnamese Montagnards, primitive mountain tribesmen who used spears and bows and arrows, as scouts and border guards along this route. Paid as mercenaries, they were armed with modern weapons and light machine guns, and fought far more fiercely than the ARVN.

Ho was unhappy about the new dimension of American involvement in South Vietnam, but Viet Cong leaders assured him that no amount of U.S. help could save the Diem regime. Not only was it hated by the peasants, but the civil and military bureaucracies in Saigon were furious at the high-handed way in which members of Diem's family ran things. Madame Nhu, sardonically nicknamed "Dragon Lady" by American correspondents, had even forced the Saigon legislature to pass a law making paired dancing illegal. Buddhist leaders were also incensed over Catholic favoritism practised by Diem.

The Viet Cong demonstrated their control of the countryside by kidnapping and killing thousands of Diem's village administrators and other Saigon appointees.

When some American newsmen reported a rising tide of revolt against the repressive Diem regime, the dictator angrily threw them out of the country. Then in February 1962 a group of young army officers attempted a second coup. Two planes of Diem's own air force bombed and strafed his palace.

DIEM WAS ABLE TO CRUSH the uprising, but it was clear that his dictatorship was in serious trouble. In Hanoi French journalist Bernard Fall talked to Ho and Dong about it.

"He is unpopular," Dong said, "and the more unpopular he is the more American aid he will require to stay in power. And the more American aid he receives, the more he will look like a puppet of the Americans, and the less likely he is to win popular support for his side."

Nevertheless, Fall pointed out, as long as the Saigon regime continued to get the full backing of the United States, was it realistic to expect it to be overthrown?

"It took us eight years of bitter fighting to defeat you French in Indo-China," Ho Chi Minh replied. "And you knew the country and had some old friendships here. Now, the South Vietnamese regime is well-armed and helped by the Americans. . . . So it may take perhaps ten years to do it, but our heroic compatriots in the South will defeat them in the end."

He added quietly, "I think the Americans greatly underestimate the determination of the Vietnamese people."

He was less responsive about his own problems. When correspondents asked him whether Hanoi was moving closer to Moscow or Peking in the widening split between the Communist super-powers, Ho replied politely but firmly, "These are problems for discussion among Socialists."

He continued to restrain both the pro-Russian and pro-Chinese factions in his cabinet. All over North Vietnam posters showed a group picture of Ho, Mao Tse-tung and Khrushchev—with Uncle Ho carefully in the middle.

Mao was irked by Ho's refusal to commit Hanoi to Red China. Visited by a French deputy who was planning to see Ho next for a study he was making of Asian Communism, Mao said, "Why go to Vietnam? It's not too good down there. You'd do better to go to North Korea. There the people are serious about solving Socialist problems the *right* way."

All through 1962 Ho sought to influence world opinion against the American intervention in Vietnam. He made himself readily available to visiting foreign officials and journalists. They were greatly impressed by the fragile but sprightly little seventy-two-year-old leader who could talk to them in French, English, German, Russian, Czech, Japanese, Portuguese and several dialects of Chinese and Vietnamese.

They admired, too, Ho's many sides as poet, painter, philosopher, revolutionary, wit, patriarch and nationalist. His ascetic way of life offered a sharp contrast to the personal greed of the luxury-loving Saigon leaders. Ho still lived in the gardener's cottage behind the Puginier Palace, where he tended the flowers and ate nothing but rice.

Looking like an impish Chinese ivory miniature, he still dressed simply in rubber-tire sandals held on by rope, and an old tunic or frayed field jacket. His salary was ten times as much as the average Vietnamese earned, but still only $840 a year. His only personal indulgence was a fondness for English and American cigarettes.

Despite his basic modesty, Ho had a secret streak of vanity. Given a book that had a sketch of him in it, he thumbed its pages rapidly to find the picture, expressing his hope that the artist had portrayed his wispy Asian beard accurately. Then he beamed, "Yes, that is very good. That looks very much like me." He sent a bouquet of flowers to the artist.

Pressed to clear up mysteries about his past, Ho would only chuckle, "Wait until I'm dead. Then you can write whatever you want about me." His personal charm was enhanced by a spirit of fun that made him enormously likable.

Journalists were allowed to move about freely to observe conditions in North Vietnam. "An austere land with austere people," reported one European correspondent. The people worked from dawn to dusk. Few could afford the Russian cameras, French bikes, Czech shoes and Bulgarian sausages on sale in Hanoi's big department store. These were little more than a promise for the future.

Clothing was rationed to three yards of material a year per person. It took two weeks of work to buy a pair of shoes, half a week's work to buy a Chinese T-shirt. If the average worker in Hanoi was not well-fed, neither did he starve. Everyone received a monthly thirty-pound rice ration. Eggs, vegetables, ducks and fruit were plentiful in the marketplace.

The old Hanoi of the French had vanished. There were no cars in the streets. Stucco villas were in disrepair, shops boarded up, broad avenues empty and pitted. Ho had more urgent uses for the billion dollars in aid he was receiving from the Russians and the Chinese.

He was harnessing his people's energies in a five-year program to transform agriculturally poor but minerally rich North Vietnam into an industrial nation. If his hopes were realized, his country would be able to supply industrial goods to all the agricultural nations of Southeast Asia.

Chemical plants had sprung up at Viet-Tri, an iron and steel center at Thai Nguyen, a tungsten mine and ore refinery at Pia-Quac, a textile industry in Nam Dinh. All were operated by North Vietnamese engineers trained in Russia, Red China and East Germany. Each factory opened with a double shift—one worker operating a machine and an apprentice at his elbow, learning, in preparation for staffing the next factory to open.

Ho explained to his people that such giant industrial steps forward required great sacrifices by everyone. Workers were regimented by Street Committees, who alone could authorize absences, and who turned everyone out for early morning gymnastics to promote physical fitness. Factory and Collective Committees set stiff work quotas, calling to account those who failed to meet them. Young Pioneers, children's groups, were encouraged to report citizens who "sabotaged" the national effort in any way. Workers who lost or damaged tools were fined for carelessness.

Some journalists saw Ho's emerging industrial nation as an enormous, busy beehive in which the production of honey was everything, the bees nothing. But the people, far from resenting such "Big Brother" regimentation, accepted it as a patriotic necessity. Did not Uncle Ho live simply and sparely, too? Had he not spent most of his life in hiding, in caves and dungeons, to free their country from the French?

He called upon them now to match his sacrifices, for a brighter tomorrow for themselves and their children, and they were determined not to fail him.

Widespread hatred was aroused, both in the North and in the South, by the tortures Diem's soldiers practiced on any Vietnamese suspected of being a Viet Cong. American correspondents witnessed prisoners beaten, kicked, tortured and drowned to make them "talk." In July 1962 the *New York Times* noted, "Improved treatment of prisoners, now marked by brutality, is an objective of the United States." Yet American military advisers present at such savage interrogations made no move to interfere or protest.

By this time it was clear that the Geneva Accords were a dead letter. The ICC issued a gloomy report in June revealing that the accords were now being violated by all parties —Saigon, Washington *and* Hanoi.

In addition to helping the Viet Cong, Ho agreed to let Giap build their North Vietnam People's Army to a force of four hundred thousand, to match the American buildup of the ARVN. These troops, armed with Soviet automatic weapons and trained to fight in swamps and jungles, were estimated by the French to be among the best combat infantry forces in the world. Better-housed than civilians, given good jobs as veterans, Giap's troops enjoyed high morale.

Ho did not expect the Americans to mount an invasion of North Vietnam. Apart from its respect for Giap's army, the American military also had to take into account the possibility that such an invasion might involve them in a full-scale land war with Red China. Ho agreed with Giap that the Pentagon was more likely instead to use its massive fleet of bombers to smash North Vietnam's factories, seeking to force Hanoi to sue for a peace settlement with Washington.

All his life Ho had preferred conciliation and compromise to the bloody waste of warfare. He now announced his willingness to sit down with any South Vietnamese regime —even Diem's—to discuss a political settlement. He was not insisting on immediate reunification of the two Vietnams, Ho declared. And he was willing to accept the verdict of any honest election that let the South Vietnamese decide their own form of government and their future.

What Ho hoped for was, at the very least, a neutral regime in Saigon that would invite the Americans to leave. He was fearful of an American decision to bomb his country, not only because of the terrible damage and loss of life, but also because it might give the Red Chinese an excuse to rush troops to his "rescue." Once enough of them had dug into North Vietnam, it would be an agonizing job getting them out.

So Ho pressed hard for a political solution in Saigon that would end the turmoil in South Vietnam—a coalition cabinet representing all factions, including the NLF.

In March 1963 Secretary of State Dean Rusk announced that the struggle against the Viet Cong was "turning an important corner," and that Diem's forces, however unpopular, "clearly have the initiative in most areas of the country."

But by May there were Buddhist demonstrations against Diem in Hué. ARVN troops opened fire, killing nine monks. Some monks began setting themselves on fire in the public squares of Saigon. Madame Nhu scoffed at these bizarre self-sacrificial protests as "monk barbecue shows." Her husband's Special Forces raided Buddhist pagodas, killing scores of monks and jailing hundreds. All Vietnam was appalled.

The world press expressed indignation. Many Saigon officials abroad, including Madame Nhu's own father, resigned in protest. South Vietnamese students joined huge new Buddhist demonstrations. Diem closed all the schools and universities, and Nhu's police arrested four thousand students.

Watching from Hanoi, Ho told Dong that the end was near for Diem. Washington could no longer afford to be associated with such a brutal dictatorship. Either the Diem regime would have to be cleaned up or replaced, or the United States would have to withdraw from South Vietnam and concede that its support of Diem had been a serious blunder.

President Kennedy recalled the American ambassador to Saigon, Frederick E. Nolting, Jr., who had been closely identified with the Diem regime. Nolting's successor, Republican Henry Cabot Lodge, demanded that Diem fire the hated Nhus and end the persecution of Buddhists and students.

Diem flatly refused.

Kenneth O'Donnell, a chief adviser to the president, later

revealed that Kennedy had by this point decided upon a complete military withdrawal from Vietnam. He had become almost totally disillusioned with the Pentagon's advice, which General Douglas MacArthur had earlier cautioned him against. MacArthur had implored Kennedy to avoid a U.S. military buildup in Vietnam or anywhere on the Asian mainland, urging the president to give priority instead to domestic problems.

Kennedy told Senator Mike Mansfield, Senate majority leader, that he planned to end America's involvement in Vietnam after he was re-elected in 1964. To try to do so sooner, he feared, would provoke a Republican campaign accusing him of "appeasing Communism." He told Mansfield, "If I tried to pull out completely now, we'd have another Joe McCarthy red scare on our hands."

On September 2, 1963, Kennedy attacked the Diem regime for having "gotten out of touch with the people." He pointed out, "In the final analysis it's their war. They are the ones who will win it or lose it. We can help them, we can give them equipment, we can send our men out there as advisers, but they have to win it."

In Saigon Diem furiously accused the CIA of plotting with South Vietnam's Buddhists to overthrow him. There was, indeed, a coup in the making, but the plotters belonged to a military junta led by General Duong Van ("Big") Minh.

The Pentagon doggedly continued to insist that all was well. Pacific fleet commander Harry D. Felt predicted victory by 1966. General Maxwell Taylor and Secretary of Defense MacNamara returned from an inspection tour with a glowing progress report. On October 3 the National Security Council reflected their optimism in a conference with Kennedy.

But the skeptical Mansfield made his own tour of Vietnam, and found that in the eight years of the Diem regime not even a start had been made in solving South Vietnam's real problems or in pacifying the countryside. Conditions were actually far worse than they had been in 1955.

"The reports of progress," Mansfield later said acidly, "are strewn like burned-out tanks all along the road which has led [us] ever more deeply into Vietnam."

On November 1 the serviceman's newspaper, *Stars and Stripes*, appeared in South Vietnam with a message from U.S. General Paul Harkins. "Victory in the sense it would apply to this kind of war is just months away," he declared, "and the reduction of American advisors can begin any time now."

That same afternoon the Diem government was overthrown.

General Minh and his fellow plotters seized the palace, arresting Diem and Nhu. Diem was shot in the truck taking him to prison by one of the rebel officers, who pronounced it "accidental suicide." Next day Nhu was killed "trying to escape." Madame Nhu, who had gone to Washington to denounce the Kennedy administration, furiously charged that her husband and brother-in-law had been "treacherously killed with either the official or unofficial blessing of the American Government."

Former President Eisenhower, who suspected the hand of the CIA in Minh's coup, checked with Ambassador Lodge, who assured him that the CIA had not been involved.

The downfall of the Diem regime caused widespread rejoicing in South Vietnam. The Viet Cong were quick to take credit for their role in ending the dictatorship, and won even wider influence over the countryside. In Hanoi Dong and Giap were jubilant, but they found Ho in a reflective mood.

As long as the Diem family had been in control of Saigon with American support, he pointed out, Hanoi could count on the hatred of the South Vietnamese for both the Diem regime and the Americans. But what if the new Minh regime were now to introduce land reform, some political freedom and honest government?

The Minh regime did not last long, however, and ten different governments came and went in Saigon during the next eighteen months. From week to week it became almost impossible to determine who was running the Saigon bureaucracy if, indeed, it was being run at all. Washington gave up trying to stabilize any regime, and concentrated instead on working with the ARVN military in prosecuting the war.

American Special Forces—the Green Berets—were trained to teach terrorist tactics to native anti-Communist forces. One Green Beret veteran, Sergeant Donald Duncan, later reported that an instructor ordered his unit not to interfere with or report any ARVN atrocity murder of Vietnamese women or children because "they're all VC or at least helping them—same difference."

Many Green Berets defended ARVN atrocities as militarily justifiable because women and children often set the booby traps that wounded and killed American and ARVN troops. California Senator Alan Cranston later revealed that up to twenty-five thousand American soldiers had been killed, not by front-line Viet Cong or North Vietnamese troops, but by mines and booby traps planted by South Vietnamese peasants.

Senator Cranston did not make this point to justify atrocities against civilians, but rather to emphasize that the South Vietnamese people simply wanted the Americans to get out of their land and stop devastating it.

Some Green Berets were sickened by the murder of villagers in the name of "fighting Communism." One told Sergeant Duncan cynically, "Except for getting a lot of people killed, all we've accomplished is making some Saigon merchants richer and some province chiefs fatter."

In the same month that Diem had been overthrown and murdered, President John F. Kennedy was assassinated in Dallas. The new president, Lyndon B. Johnson, quickly threw his support behind the new Minh regime, setting America's goal in South Vietnam as an unqualified military victory.

He stepped up the flow of money and weapons to Saigon. Most of the aid wound up, as usual, in the pockets of the military and their political allies. Ironically, much of the American goods that was diverted for profit into the black market found its way into Viet Cong hands.

In a hearing of the Ninetieth Congress, Representative Otto E. Passman angrily pointed out that ARVN soldiers who had been privates ten years earlier were now generals "going from bicycles to Cadillacs . . . from rice shacks to palatial homes on the coast."

President Johnson justified his escalation of the American war effort in Vietnam by insisting that Ho Chi Minh was sending North Vietnamese to fight in South Vietnam, and was the chief supplier of arms to the Viet Cong.

But on March 6, 1964, Pulitzer Prize-winning reporter David Halberstam wrote in the *New York Times*, "The war is largely a conflict of southerners fought on southern land. No capture of North Vietnamese in the South has come to light." The *Times* also reported later that a study of captured Viet Cong weapons showed that 75 percent were of American manufacture, and the other 25 percent were home-made rifles.

It was easy for the tough, dedicated VC to capture ARVN weapons. Often the ARVN fought only under pressure of their American advisers, and could rarely be trusted to carry out a mission by themselves. Most ARVN were draftees who had little incentive to risk death or disablement for a regime whose security police drove a portable guillotine from village to village to execute Viet Cong suspects.

Talk of negotiations or peace with Hanoi was a prison offense, and the jails overflowed with political prisoners. Minh's troops were also used to extract taxes for Saigon and rents for the landlords. Not surprisingly, in 1964 fully one hundred thousand of the three hundred thousand-man ARVN army deserted.

This was why President Johnson was rapidly coming to the conclusion that if there were to be a military victory in Vietnam, to save American prestige, it would have to be won with American troops. That belief was to plunge the United States into its gravest domestic crisis since the Civil War.

Fighting the Americans

GENERAL WILLIAM C. WESTMORELAND took over command of the U.S. military advisers, now a force of twenty-three thousand, in July. He was chagrined to find a miserable military situation that did not correspond with the optimistic reports being given to the American public by the Johnson Administration. In fact, over 80 percent of the supposedly "secured" hamlets were actually cooperating instead with the Viet Cong.

The VC were a well-organized, disciplined revolutionary army of some one hundred thirty-two thousand, mostly peasants who farmed by day and carried out sabotage missions by night. Over 80 percent were guerrillas fighting in the areas where they had been born. Overall military strategy was blueprinted by General Giap in Hanoi and communicated over a secret radio network, but the VC made their own tactical decisions locally.

Many of the rank-and-file guerrillas had never heard of Karl Marx and had little conception of Communism, except that Uncle Ho said it was a good thing, which was reason enough for them to support it. Communism, Ho told them, had already made wonderful changes in the lives of the North Vietnamese.

Over 80 percent of the peasants under Ho no longer worked for landlords, but owned shares in collective farms. All villages in the Red River delta region, and four out of five mountain villages, now had medical stations. Smallpox, cholera, and polio, once dread diseases, had been wiped out, and TB and malaria drastically reduced. Infant mortality, 30 percent under the French, was now less than 3 percent.

Did not the Viet Cong want such progress for themselves in South Vietnam? It would be possible, Ho promised, once the Americans were driven out like the French, and a genuine people's government came to power in Saigon.

General "Big" Minh had been overthrown by Major General Nguyen Khanh, who was now ordered by the CIA to try to get a semblance of legitimacy for his regime by holding controlled elections. Honest elections were obviously out of the question because, as Walter Lippmann explained in the *Washington Post* in April 1964, "The truth, which is being obscured for the American people, is that the Saigon government has no more than 30 percent of the people and controls (even in daylight) not much more than a quarter of the territory."

Even the U.S. Military Advisor Group newspaper in Saigon admitted that the NLF had the support of up to five million South Vietnamese, a highly conservative estimate.

General Khanh opened polling stations only in the small areas controlled by Saigon. Even so, the only candidates permitted to run for office were those approved by the Saigon military junta. The NLF, branding the election a farce, called upon the South Vietnamese to boycott it.

Saigon threatened that anyone who could not produce a card showing he had voted would lose his rice rations. Soldiers and police rounded up voters, driving them in military trucks to polling stations. An Associated Press correspondent reported that in one province, over a million more votes were counted than there were voters.

Khanh's regime claimed an "overwhelming victory." President Johnson declared that these elections gave the world a "lesson in democracy." Some administration supporters, conceding that the elections had been fraudulent, argued that there had never been any honest elections in all of Indo-China anyhow.

On July 30 South Vietnamese naval boats raided radar and naval installations on North Vietnamese islands. Three days later a U.S. destroyer was sent on patrol near the islands in the international waters of the Gulf of Tonkin.

The Defense Department then reported that the ship had been attacked by North Vietnamese PT boats, which had been driven off by gunfire. Washington protested to Hanoi.

Five days later the Defense Department reported a second attack on the U.S. destroyers *Maddox* and *Turner Joy* by the PT boats. On August 5 President Johnson ordered North Vietnam's naval bases bombed in retaliation. He then asked Congress for a joint resolution "to promote the maintenance of international peace and security in Southeast Asia."

Sending Defense Department officials to brief the Senate

Foreign Relations Committee on the PT boat attacks, the president asked Congress to authorize him "to take all necessary measures to repel any armed attacks against the forces of the United States and to prevent further aggression."

Senator William Fulbright, Chairman of the Foreign Relations Committee, had been vehemently opposed to American involvement in Vietnam. Now, however, he reluctantly agreed to sponsor the Gulf of Tonkin Resolution. It passed both houses of Congress almost unanimously, opposed only by Senators Wayne Morse and Ernest Gruening. They branded the resolution a blank check to make war without consulting Congress.

A later investigation heard officers of the *Maddox* reveal that the North Vietnamese PT boats had *not* fired any shells or torpedoes at the American destroyers. Fulbright, infuriated, accused the Defense Department of having deliberately lied to his committee about the alleged attacks.

But President Johnson, armed with the Gulf of Tonkin Resolution, prepared to bomb North Vietnam and to build up large American military forces in South Vietnam. He was convinced that by Americanizing and escalating the war he would soon bring both Ho and the Viet Cong to terms.

These plans, however, could not be revealed until after the 1964 elections. Running for a presidential term in his own right, Johnson assured voters that he had no intention of allowing the United States to get bogged down in a land war in Southeast Asia, or to engage in any rash actions. He castigated his opponent, Republican Senator Barry Goldwater, as an irresponsible torchbearer for the hawks.

"They call upon us to supply American boys to do the job that Asian boys should do," Johnson declared on August 12. "They ask us to take reckless action which might risk the lives of millions and engulf much of Asia and certainly threaten the peace of the world. Moreover such action would offer no solution at all to the real problem of Vietnam."

On October 21, in Akron, Ohio, he repeated his pledge that American boys would not be sent to fight in Vietnam. He also told voters that he was watching for "any signal" from Hanoi that Ho Chi Minh was interested in negotiating an end to the war, and that he would "go anywhere and do anything" for "unconditional" peace talks on Vietnam.

Meeting with U Thant, who had been trying for several years to end the bloodshed in Southeast Asia, Johnson agreed to the UN secretary general's plan to approach Ho Chi Minh privately, through the Russians, for secret peace talks in Burma. Ho, faced with the threat of having his whole country laid waste by American bombing, quickly sent word that he would be glad to send a peace envoy to Burma.

U Thant told UN Ambassador Adlai Stevenson, who was delighted and rushed word to the president. There was no reply. Puzzled, U Thant and Stevenson could only assume that the president feared to bring up the issue before the elections were over. But even after Johnson had won another four years in the White House, there was still no reply.

When Stevenson pressed for an answer, Secretary Mac-Namara simply told him that the administration had made its own private inquiry, and did not believe that Ho Chi

Minh was seriously interested in peace. U Thant investigated. He found that the State Department's only soundings had been made with the Canadian representative of the ICC in Hanoi, who had merely expressed an opinion, and had no direct access to Ho of any kind.

Stevenson and U Thant then decided to persist on their own. Making arrangements for peace talks in Burma, they won confirmation from Ho that he would send an envoy. In January 1965 Stevenson told the White House. Again, silence.

Finally Stevenson was told that Washington could not participate in peace talks because just the rumor of such a meeting would be enough to topple the shaky Saigon government. U Thant was forced to give up and report to Ho that the Americans, despite all of Johnson's campaign speeches, were not interested in negotiating a peace.

Twenty-four hours after Ho received Thant's message, the American bombing of North Vietnam began.

U Thant, depressed by his failure and shocked by the bombings, made a speech in February 1965 stating that the real problem in Vietnam was basically one of a people fighting for their independence. He called for a return to the Geneva Accords. Then he dropped a bombshell by stating that the American people were not getting the whole truth.

The *New York Times* broke the story of the Johnson administration's refusal to agree to peace talks. The State Department denied the charge. Later in the year, however, when revelations by Stevenson confirmed U Thant's charges, the State Department was compelled to admit the truth.

Such attempts to mislead the public, added to the president's broken promises not to send combat troops to Vietnam, created what the press began to call sarcastically the administration's "credibility gap."

To defend their policies, President Johnson and Secretary of State Dean Rusk doggedly insisted that North Vietnam was guilty of committing aggression against South Vietnam, a SEATO ally, which Washington had a commitment to defend.

Ho denied the charge. Vietnam was a single nation, he maintained. The Saigon regime was an artificial creation by the Americans, whose intervention had violated the Geneva Accords and prevented reunification of the country. The only aliens in South Vietnam, Ho pointed out, were Americans and a few token forces wrung out of some allies.

But his tone was not belligerent. He was in no hurry for reunification, Ho declared, and he announced that the North had no wish to meddle in affairs of the South. "We have enough problems in the North alone," he said.

He did not say so, but he was under heavy pressure from the Russians to make concessions to the Americans in order to bring about peace negotiations. There were new leaders now in the Soviet Union. Khrushchev had been deposed, and the new Soviet premier, Aleksei Kosygin, came to Hanoi to persuade Ho to go along with the new soft line in Moscow.

Kosygin's mission angered Truong Chinh and the pro-Chinese faction in Ho's cabinet. They pressed Ho to adopt Mao Tse-tung's rigid hostility toward Washington.

On the same day that Kosygin arrived in Hanoi, the Viet Cong in the south launched a fierce attack on the American base at Pleiku. There was speculation as to its timing. Did the Viet Cong mean to warn Ho not to negotiate with the Russians over their heads, at their expense?

On February 7, in retaliation, American bombers began striking North Vietnam in massive raids. The first bombs fell on Hanoi while Kosygin was there urging conciliation of Washington. It was a political blunder by the United States of enormous magnitude. Two days later a white-faced Kosygin angrily announced a program of increased Soviet aid for North Vietnam.

Ho's people were badly frightened by the noise of the bombers, the explosions and anti-aircraft fire. They sought refuge in shelters and jumped into garden trenches to escape the shrapnel raining down on the pavements. Ambulances sped about the city picking up the wounded, many of whom were children, and rushing them to crowded hospitals.

Ho ordered Hanoi evacuated as quickly as possible by women, children and non-essential workers. The population rapidly dwindled by hundreds of thousands until it was down to only a fourth of its normal one million two hundred thousand people. Ho changed working shifts to early morning and late evening hours, to lessen the danger from midday air raids.

Hanoi began to take on the aspect of a ghost town.

"You hear the shuffle of feet," said one visitor, "but no squabbling of merchants, no squeals, no laughter. They don't even seem to talk to one another. You can hear the birds singing downtown at midday. It is oddly saddening."

Ho worried that the American bombers might accidentally hit the dikes that protected the populous Red River Valley, and parts of Hanoi itself, from floods. He did not believe that Washington would deliberately bring about the mass drowning and starvation of civilians in the North's most heavily populated areas, as the Germans did in World War II when they bombed the dikes of Holland.

Ho appealed to the youth of his country to prepare to take their place in a patriotic struggle that might last as long as their own lives. Hanoi's teenagers flocked into training squads—boys with wooden rifles, girls with mock grenades. Their schools were adorned with Ho's motto: "Though your clothes may be soiled, keep your honor unspotted."

Meanwhile the war in the south grew more savage.

American correspondents reported widespread atrocities committed by ARVN troops to make captives and suspects talk. ARVN soldiers tied captured Viet Cong to armored trucks and pulled them through rivers. Suspects were whipped and kicked while their wives and children looked on in terror. Some VC prisoners were thrown alive out of flying helicopters or dangled by their feet from the copters to frighten them into talking.

"Who among us knew enough to be shocked," asked famous American playwright Arthur Miller in January 1965, "let alone protest, at the photographs of the Vietnamese torturing Vietcong prisoners which our press has published? The Vietnamese are wearing United States equipment, are paid by us, and could not torture without us. There is no way around this—the prisoner crying out in agony is *our* prisoner."

But the Viet Cong also committed atrocities, primarily against hamlet chiefs who had bought their appointments from the Saigon military. To intimidate the three to four thousand hamlets cooperating with Saigon, the Viet Cong kidnapped, murdered and mutilated village officials and their families. The VC also blew up buses along Saigon-controlled highways.

American officials in Saigon distributed pamphlets through the countryside charging the Viet Cong with these atrocities, while remaining silent on those committed by the ARVN. This propaganda largely backfired, however, because the Viet Cong's chief victims were hated by the villagers they exploited, and the VC were often regarded as Robin Hoods.

The South Vietnamese were also less angered by the VC's blowing up buses than impressed with their ability to control even the main highways. Ho was amused at how poorly the Americans understood the thinking of his people.

The American Special Forces tried to help their field officers understand this thinking in secret bulletins they warned must not be seen by Saigon officials. The bulletins explained that over 70 percent of the countryside was sympathetic to the Viet Cong, providing them with food, shelter and recruits, and giving them military information.

These peasants resented Saigon-appointed village chiefs as outsiders. They were not necessarily pro-Communist, but they respected the NLF as a coalition of all nationalist groups, and would not cooperate with or fight for Saigon unless forced to by the ARVN. Such revelations made some of the American field officers wonder about the sense of supporting a regime so unpopular with its own people.

Ho's spies reported to him that Marine combat divisions were making massive landings at Cam Ranh Bay in South Vietnam, and that it was being developed into a major military base. At the time Le Duan had only a cadre of five hundred North Vietnamese fighting with the South Vietnamese VC below the Seventeenth Parallel—far fewer than the twenty thousand American military advisers with the ARVN.

Yet it was to counter this "aggression" from the north that the Johnson administration began sending to South Vietnam an expeditionary force that would soon number well over half a million American troops in the field.

At the same time American bombers began hitting North Vietnamese supply staging areas, communication routes and other military targets. Many bombers were shot down by accurate surface-to-air SAM missiles supplied to Ho by the Soviet Union.

American ground forces now took over the main burden of the combat against the Viet Cong, despite President Kennedy's warning that the South Vietnamese had to win their own war, and that if it ever became a white man's war the Americans would lose it as the French had lost it before them.

It seemed at first that an American victory was inevitable. How could the Viet Cong or Ho stand up against billions of dollars' worth of the most sophisticated military equipment, backed up by massive U.S. wealth and an army equipped with vastly superior fire power?

No longer mere "spectators" in the war, American forces fanned out from seacoast bases in "search and destroy" missions against Viet Cong strongholds. The marines were photographed by TV newsmen setting fire to the thatched huts of villages "suspected" of helping the VC, or from which there had been sniper fire. If the villagers had not been VC sympathizers before such missions, they were afterwards.

On April 7, 1965, President Johnson declared at Johns Hopkins University that Americans were in Vietnam "to strengthen world order . . . to slow down aggression . . . to improve the life of man in that conflict-torn corner of the world."

As an inducement to Ho and the Viet Cong to yield, the president promised that the United States would pay half the cost of a $2 billion plan to develop the Mekong River basin for all of Southeast Asia. He declared his willingness to enter "unconditional negotiations" to end the war.

Ho took a sardonic view of the Johnson technique of holding out a carrot to his adversaries while he beat them with a stick. The United States could obtain "peace with honor," Ho replied, only if it withdrew its troops from South Vietnam, ended its bombing raids on the North, and permitted the country to reunite without interference. Otherwise he was prepared for total war, for as long as the Americans persisted.

"We have been fighting for our independence for more than twenty-five years, and of course we cherish peace," Ho declared. "But we will never surrender our independence to purchase peace with the United States."

He fully expected that before the war was over, Hanoi and the port city of Haiphong would be leveled to the ground. He was prepared to retreat to the caves in the hills north of Hanoi, and continue fighting from there as he once had against the French. Sooner or later, he told Dong, the Americans would be forced to come to terms with Moscow and Peking, who could not allow North Vietnam to be destroyed.

But meanwhile his whole country was under devastating attacks from the American bombers filling the skies north of the Seventeenth Parallel. To remain invisible to the raiders and their observation planes, peasants camouflaged their green-painted bikes and wore banana branches in their hats.

In five months American bombers smashed 30 North Vietnamese bases, hit 127 anti-aircraft batteries, shattered 34 bridges, destroyed 34 truck and train convoys. How long could Ho hold out at that rate?

12

"I Want Some Coonskins On the Wall!"

HE MOBILIZED TWO AND A HALF MILLION young men and women into a "Brigade of Young Volunteers to Fight U.S. Aggression for National Salvation." After group gymnastics at 5:00 A.M. they replaced militiamen in fields and factories, working long hours with time out for educational courses.

Ho was wryly amused when he read an interview with the new premier of South Vietnam, named by the military junta in Saigon on June 19, 1965. General Nguyen Cao Ky was asked by a correspondent to name the historical figure he most admired. Ky had replied, to Washington's horror, "Adolph Hitler."

Emissaries Clark Clifford and Professor Henry Kissinger, sent by the White House to evaluate Ky's government, found it just another crude Saigon dictatorship that siphoned off American aid into graft for the army officer class and the bureaucrats, who were promoted, not punished, for theft.

Once more U Thant appealed to both Hanoi and Washington for negotiations to end the war. President Johnson laid down two conditions. Ho Chi Minh had to accept South Vietnam as a separate, independent state, and had to agree to pull all North Vietnamese forces out of the South.

Ho felt these demands required him to repudiate the Geneva Accords, abandon the Viet Cong and leave the American military in control of South Vietnam. He rejected Johnson's ultimatum flatly, as the president had expected.

Negotiations at that time were the last thing Washington wanted, with Saigon controlling less than 20 percent of South Vietnam, and Westmoreland privately reporting that the Viet Cong were defeating the ARVN everywhere.

Now Johnson ordered the marines to push out of their coastal enclaves, under umbrellas of heavy support, and to engage and crush the Viet Cong. But the guerrilla forces, warned of American attacks well in advance by the peasants, had usually melted away long before the marines reached their positions. The exasperated marines would turn "liberated" hamlets over to the ARVN to hold, and push on.

The ARVN would promptly loot, collect taxes and seize the lands the Viet Cong had distributed. In short order the Viet Cong would reappear, drive out the ARVN with the aid of the peasants, and return the area to the underground government of the NLF.

American air and naval gun attacks, in support of the marine assaults, did fearsome damage to the people of the countryside and their villages. In just two hamlets, over one hundred peasants were killed by bomb and shell fragments, and several hundred were wounded. In a hamlet whose people depended upon a coconut plantation, the groves were wiped out by a supporting naval bombardment from offshore.

Soon some four million refugees, a third of South Vietnam's rural population, were fleeing the regions under attack. The American military reported that they were "escaping" from Communist-held territory to the protection of refugee camps set up by the American forces. But in Senate testimony on September 30, 1965, Roger Hilsman, a former assistant secretary of state, admitted that they were homeless because of "American bombings and shelling."

"To bomb a village, even though the guerrillas are using it as a base for sniping, will recruit more Viet Cong than are killed," Hilsman testified. "If bombing the North has been a bad mistake, bombing the South has been a tragic one—for it has worked to alienate the people."

Ho was sick at heart to see the devastation of his country, North and South alike, by America's vast military might. But he knew that the bombings were uniting his people solidly behind him, just as the British had rallied behind Churchill during the Nazi blitz of London. The bombings were also horrifying millions of Americans.

Many were raising their voices in angry protest.

"The actions of the United States in Vietnam," declared a Lawyers' Committee on American Policy Toward Vietnam, "contravene the essential provisions of the United Nations Charter, to which we are bound by treaty; violate the Geneva Accords, which we pledged to observe; are not sanctioned by the treaty creating [SEATO]; and violate our own Constitution . . . by the prosecution of the war in Vietnam without a Congressional declaration of war."

The Lawyers' Committee called the Vietnam conflict a civil war in which North Vietnamese forces did not constitute foreign intervention, whereas the presence of American troops did.

Peking, as the major power closest to North Vietnam, saw the Americans as concerned less with crushing Ho Chi Minh than with containing Red China's influence in Asia and revolutionary movements everywhere.

By November 1965 American protests against the war were beginning to rise to a roar. After six months on the job as deputy director of the United States AID mission to Saigon, J. H. Edwards quit, writing Washington, "I don't like, nor approve what we are doing here. It is at the same time both unconscious and unconscionable."

When *New York Times* correspondent Harrison Salisbury visited North Vietnam, he was startled to witness patriotic parades in which banners were carried praising "the good and peace-loving people of the United States." Ho was impressed by the turbulent anti-war demonstrations mounted by American doves. Overestimating the strength of the peace movement, he reported their protests to his people as proof that the American people would soon force their government out of Vietnam.

But meanwhile his tiny country shook under the crashing of more bombs than had been dropped during all of World War II. Hundreds of thousands of men, women and children were killed and mutilated by napalm, phosphorus, magnesium and steel-pellet explosives. Ho did not believe that the B-52 strategic bombers deliberately aimed at civilian targets. But many homes, schools and hospitals were close to strategic roads, bridges and factories. And by the end of 1965 whole areas of North Vietnam were beginning to look from the air like the cratered surface of the moon.

Hanoi itself, once the liveliest center of French culture in Southeast Asia, was now a city of boarded-up shops and restaurants. By nine at night its streets were deserted and dark to save electricity, with the only sound to be heard the chirping of crickets in the tamarind trees.

Through the daylight hours, because of the fear of the bombers, practically nothing on four wheels moved along North Vietnam's roads. The countryside presented the illusion of a rural nation at peace. Peasants spread thatch to dry, threshed rice in courtyards, dyed grass reeds for weaving baskets. But as night fell, roads and forest paths came alive with camouflaged bike and truck convoys carrying supplies southward.

Bombed-out bridges were replaced with bamboo raft pontoons, or with ferries pulled across rivers along cables. The Ham Rong bridge, spanning a narrow valley between two steep mountains, had been the target of a hundred raids by an estimated thousand bombers. An important supply link, it was no sooner hit than repaired. Ho praised the workers of Ham Rong as a symbol of North Vietnamese defiance and persistence that no amount of military power could crush.

British correspondent James Cameron asked Ho if he really thought that he could defeat the United States.

"I've got used to being an old revolutionary," Ho said smiling. "The one thing old revolutionaries have to be is optimistic. You wait and see."

The more the Americans bombed, the more plaster casts of Uncle Ho the people of Vietnam bought for their homes. He was never personally blamed for their hardships; all

grievances were directed at "the government." They revered Ho as a saintly patriot, a popular uncle who genu-
inely cared for his people and wisely did only what was best
for them.

American soldiers, searching the bodies of dead Viet
Cong and North Vietnamese, were astonished at how often
they found in wallets pictures of Uncle Ho, along with pictures of the dead men's families and children.

Now seventy-six, Ho left the actual running of the country more and more to his trusted aide of over forty years,
Premier Pham Van Dong, while he devoted himself to
major decisions.

Dong told James Cameron, "Of course we can't vanquish
the United States. That would be fantasy, and we are not
talking in terms of fantasy. We're not *trying* to vanquish the
United States. There seems to be some preposterous belief
in America that we are threatening them—a poverty-
stricken little country like Vietnam threatening the most
powerful nation on earth! We are trying to get *rid* of them.
They're on our soil, and we don't want them there. Let
them go away and the war is over."

He asked, "How many Russian soldiers have you seen
here? Not one. . . . How many Chinese soldiers have you
seen? Not one. Maybe a few technicians. . . . If I were an
American young man I wouldn't want to fight here either.
The whole situation is nonsensical and wretched!"

Ho grew concerned when Moscow and Peking began to
quarrel over how Soviet supplies should reach him. China
wanted them sent by sea in Russian ships, because shipping
them overland by Chinese railroads might provoke an
American air attack. The Russians insisted they cross China

by rail, fearing a U.S. decision to bomb or blockade Haiphong.

Dong and Giap urged Ho to back Moscow's position.
Chinh, along with Le Duan, argued for Peking's point of
view. Ho remained firm in his refusal to take sides.

Chou En-lai visited Hanoi to urge closer Peking-Hanoi
ties at a Lao Dong party convention. Ho, sitting on the
stage behind him, sabotaged the Chinese leader's appeal by
subtly aping Chou's dramatic facial gestures as he spoke, to
the delegates' amusement and Chou's bewilderment.

As a result of Ho's shrewd neutrality, the North Vietnamese Army continued, while feeding largely on Chinese
rice, to be equipped with Chinese and Soviet infantry
weapons, Russian SAM missiles and Czech artillery.

Ho now acknowledged that he, in turn, was supplying
heavy arms to the Viet Cong and directing their overall
strategy. "One cannot remain a spectator," he declared.

On December 10, 1965, he read that President Johnson
was willing to have the views of the NLF heard at any
peace negotiations, but that the NLF itself could not be
accorded any recognition that might lead to the formation
of a coalition government for South Vietnam. To Ho this
meant that the only peace Washington was willing to consider would be one which kept the Saigon dictatorship in
power.

In reply, Ho told his old friend Sainteny, who visited him
in January 1966, that any talks with the United States
would have to be preceded by an end to the bombing and
by recognition of the NLF. Whatever Ho said on the record
to a Western diplomat, he knew, would find its way back to
the State Department as, indeed, it was meant to do.

Sainteny found him rosy-cheeked and in cheerful spirits, his sense of humor as lively as ever. Ho enjoyed wandering around the countryside, his trousers rolled up like a rice paddy worker's, talking to peasants who didn't recognize him. He also liked to speak briefly to workers at factory, collective and street committee meetings, afterwards distributing oranges or candies to children, and cigarettes to adults.

Ho's physician had told him to stop smoking, but he only sighed, "When you are as old as I am, you don't worry about the harm of cigarettes any more."

On January 28, 1966, Senator William Fulbright began televised hearings of the Senate Foreign Relations Committee on the war. His purpose was to inform the American people of facts which the Johnson administration was keeping from them.

Military experts like former marine generals James Gavin and David M. Shoup explained why the president's escalation of the war was a tragic mistake. Noted psychiatrists testified that the administration was suffering from a "cold war psychosis" which, in seeing little North Vietnam as a threat, amounted to "national schizophrenia." Fulbright stung the president by charging that instead of making America "the Great Society," as he had promised, his obsession with Vietnam had made America "a sick society."

Ho was impressed with the Fulbright hearings, but found it difficult to understand how, given such lucid analyses on TV, the American people could continue to permit their government to persist in prosecuting the war.

Miami editor William C. Baggs was allowed to attend an Independence Day celebration in Hanoi, and was granted an interview with Ho. Baggs tried to find out what conciliatory steps Ho might take if Johnson stopped the bombing.

"The Americans talk of ending the bombings if we would make some reciprocal gesture," Ho replied. "But this would be like a person who is held up by a bandit in Chicago. And after he holds you up he wants to know what price you are willing to pay him not to shoot you."

Ho revealed honest bewilderment at America's betrayal, as he saw it, of its own traditions. "What in the world is going on in the United States?" he asked Baggs. "Your country has no history of being aggressive. I knew something about the United States. What are the people thinking? Why have you invested so much in such a large war in this little country so far away? Tell me . . . is the Statue of Liberty standing on her head?"

He assured Baggs that, despite everything, he bore no animosity toward Americans, and that when peace came, even Lyndon Johnson would be greeted with flowers as a tourist.

"We respect the American people . . . an intelligent . . . a peace-and-democracy-loving people," he said. He was regretful that Americans were being sent to Vietnam as soldiers to kill instead of as technicians to help. "This may be difficult for you to believe. I am grieved not only when the Vietnamese people are killed. I am also grieved when American soldiers are killed. I sympathize with their parents."

But he added firmly, "Not even your nuclear weapons would force us to surrender after so long and violent a struggle for the independence of our country."

Ho was convinced that, whether or not he lived to see it, sooner or later there would be another Dienbienphu, and the Americans, like the French, would be forced to depart.

At the Independence Day rally, after the crowds had sung the North Vietnamese battle hymn, "We Shall Win," Ho smoothed his white beard and smiled as he offered a gentle rebuke: "The front rows did not sing loud enough." He wanted the message of the hymn heard distinctly across the Pacific.

As 1966 wore on, the massive use of American air power only intensified the determination of the Vietnamese, North and South, to fight on. The people were outraged when Ho's deputy minister of health reported that in sixteen months of bombing, 180 hospitals and medical centers in North Vietnam had been hit. Few peasants were converted from Communism by the hundreds of tons of napalm and other bombs that were dropped on them daily from American planes.

Southern peasants also bitterly resented the use of air-sprayed chemical defoliants which destroyed rice crops and rubber trees, to eliminate "Viet Cong hiding places." A combined area the size of Connecticut was laid waste, creating widespread hunger and forcing the United States to ship rice to a country that had once exported it.

President Johnson, challenged by critics to explain exactly why the United States was fighting in Vietnam, replied in his 1966 State of the Union message that it was "because a friendly nation has asked us for help against Communist aggression. Ten years ago we pledged our help. Three Presidents have supported that pledge. We will not break it. Second, our own security is tied to the peace of Asia. Twice in one generation we have had to fight against aggression in the Far East. To ignore aggression would only increase the danger of a larger war."

But turbulent anti-war demonstrations during 1966 made it clear to the president that his Vietnam policy was highly unpopular with millions of Americans. Draft cards were burned in defiance. The White House was picketed by ten thousand dissenters. Graduates walked out of commencement ceremonies at which administration officials were honored. Church leaders denounced the war and reproached Johnson for violating his 1964 campaign promises not to bomb North Vietnam or send American boys to fight and die in an Asian war.

The president sought to pacify the dissenters by ordering a thirty-seven-day pause in the bombing of North Vietnam, inviting Ho to make a reciprocal gesture toward peace. But to Ho a "pause" in the bombing was an insulting attempt at blackmail. Did the president actually expect Hanoi to negotiate with a resumption of the bombing held over Ho's head like a Damocles' sword?

Ho coolly ignored the ploy. On February 1, 1966, Johnson ended the bombing pause and declared testily, "It seems clear that what is holding up peace in the world today is not the United States."

Five days later, in Honolulu, he met with Premier Ky and American military and civilian officials in Saigon. Henry Cabot Lodge and Edward Lansdale, who was now Lodge's aide, warned him that South Vietnam could not be secured by arms alone. The people could be won away from the Viet Cong only by being given an attractive alternative to Communism—genuine democracy and real land reform.

Johnson agreed to a new "pacification" program. Ky was forced to promise the South Vietnamese a constitution by October, and "real democratic elections in 1967"—the wording in itself a confession that the previous elections held in South Vietnam had been fraudulent.

Meeting privately with his generals at Honolulu, Johnson declared emphatically, "I want some coonskins on the wall!" It was his Texas euphemism for military victory.

He had still not given up his conviction that if he just kept escalating American power, Ho would have to surrender.

13

The Bombs Rain Down

KY WAS TOLD TO ORDER his ARVN forces to join in the "search-and-destroy" missions. But the ARVN still prudently continued to avoid making contact with the enemy whenever possible. The American forces sarcastically labelled their efforts "search-and-avoid" missions. In disgust they finally removed the ARVN from all combat situations, using them only for rear-echelon "pacification."

ARVN officers took off long weekends to enjoy their apartments and villas. Most ARVN commanders controlled the laundry, garbage, bar and brothel rackets near American installations, sharing this loot with higher-ups in the Saigon government. ARVN draftees had little respect for their officers, for whom the war was simply a way of getting rich off the Americans. Jealous and resentful, the rank-and-file "got theirs" by looting and pillaging villages.

Atrocities committed by the ARVN grew in number and fury. In February 1966 the ARVN raided Binh An and massacred 288 villagers, three-fourths of them women and children. Binh An was not unusual.

That spring, after a six-week investigation, William Pepper, director of the Center for the Study and Research of Children of the Mercy College, a New York Catholic institute, reported "25,000 children have been killed in the war since 1961, 750,000 others have been injured, disabled, or burnt by napalm. More than 10,000 are concentrated in orphanages, millions of others are living a miserable life in the refugee centers. Most of them suffer from tuberculosis or typhus. Millions of others are wandering homeless in the towns, wasting away their time in begging."

When Ho warned he might try captured American pilots as war criminals, a European correspondent pointed out that this would violate the Geneva Convention rules of warfare. Ho handed him a news report of Pepper's disclosures.

"How many American children," he asked quietly, "are North Vietnamese pilots doing *that* to?"

Heavy loads of bombs rained down daily on Hanoi and Haiphong, but many of the factories they hit were empty. Ho had already dispersed as many industries as possible to the countryside. Cave factories were now turning out spare parts for motor trucks. In underground quarters young workers operated lathes and drill presses, and medical schools trained corps of doctors and nurses.

American bombers did not spare Namdinh, North Vietnam's third largest city, demolishing everything in it but a rice mill. "For blocks and blocks I could see nothing but desolation," Harrison Salisbury reported in the *New York Times*. "Residential housing, stores, all the buildings were destroyed, damaged or abandoned. I felt that I was walking through the city of a vanished civilization."

The lone rice mill was operated by women workers who

kept rifles on the sills of open windows to fire at American planes when the air-raid siren wailed. Salisbury noticed that most workers and peasants in North Vietnam bore arms, an unusual mark of trust in a Communist country, indicating Ho's complete confidence in the support of his people. The military junta that ran the Saigon regime scarcely trusted their own troops, let alone the civilians of South Vietnam.

On July 17, 1966, Ho exhorted his people to fight on, "if need be, twenty years or more," but never to surrender to American pressure, even if Hanoi and Haiphong were destroyed like Namdinh. Now he began sending some five hundred trained guerrillas a month to join "our brothers in the South."

In the United States Senate, meanwhile, angry doves were attacking "Johnson's War" in an attempt to arouse public opinion. Senator George McGovern pointed out, "All but one of the South Vietnamese generals who represent the military junta fought with the French against their own people in the war for independence which followed World War II. Would not this be roughly comparable to having eight or nine Benedict Arnolds attempting to run the U.S. in the years that followed our own war for independence?"

Senator Frank Church declared, "I do not think Ho Chi Minh can be forced to the negotiating table on his knees—unless we drag him there in chains. . . . Until the American intervention occurred, this was a Vietnamese war between various factions of Vietnamese people. . . . It is understandable that the world should think of the Vietnamese war in terms of American intervention rather than in terms of the aggression of north against south."

When the administration insisted that the Viet Cong controlled most of South Vietnam only through terror tactics, Senate doves demanded to know why, in that case, terror tactics hadn't worked for the brutal ARVN forces.

Even Professor Wesley R. Fishel, who had led the first Michigan State University group supporting Diem, admitted, "The means that are required to achieve our ends often fall short of what we consider desirable and decent. The bombing of Communist-held villages, the use of napalm, the maltreatment of prisoners, the generally murderous character of the war, are deeply disturbing."

Sometimes marine bombers not only hit villages that cooperated with the Viet Cong, but also mistakenly bombed villages cooperating with Saigon. *New Yorker* reporter Jonathan Schell was told by the marines that in one South Vietnamese province, 70 percent of the villages had been destroyed by American bombs. He checked with a gloomy American colonel who was supposed to head a "pacification" program there.

"There are just *two* villages still standing," the colonel corrected Schell grimly, "and if anyone tells you there are more, they are liars."

By the end of 1966, defying military censorship, U.S. reporters in Vietnam were cabling home more exposés.

"Throughout the war, the Administration and the Saigon Press Corps have been natural enemies, like the cobra and the mongoose," declared AP correspondent Peter Arnett. "We were attacked by officials because what we found in Vietnam was directly contrary to most of the ideas held in Washington. At times, particularly in 1966 and 1967, there was a conscious government campaign to discredit the press corps in Vietnam in the eyes of the U.S. public."

The Associated Press revealed that the Saigon regime was saturated with black marketeering, theft, bribery, currency manipulation, and waste on an "unprecedented scale." While American troops were dying in the jungles, the AP noted, "a small minority of South Vietnamese and Americans are making a profit out of the war by at least a half million dollars daily—perhaps much more." As much as 40 percent of American aid went down the drain.

"Corruption is the overriding issue in this war," an American AID official told a *Newsweek* reporter in Saigon. "I don't see how we can talk about victory until something is done about it." But the National Police, commanded by Brigadier General Nguyen Ngoc Loan, a crony of Ky's, far from seeking to punish corruption, participated in it.

Under American pressure, Loan finally staged a "raid" on the open black market of Saigon, burning seized goods for photographers. Reporters who checked afterward found that he had burned mostly empty boxes and a few cans of food.

Loan was the South Vietnamese general who shocked Americans by proudly having his picture taken calmly shooting in the head a trussed, blindfolded prisoner kneeling in the street. When the national assembly debated who should be allowed to run for president in the future "real elections" Ky had promised, Loan stalked into the assembly, read a list of the only candidates he would allow to run, then announced crisply that the debate was over.

Life magazine reported an argument between two American officers in Saigon, one of whom insisted that no matter what his politics, Ho Chi Minh was the George Washington

of Vietnam. The other replied gloomily, "All right, so he is.
. . . But do *we* have to get stuck with all the Benedict
Arnolds?"

The Viet Cong now exercised such control over the
countryside that truck drivers had to pay them road tolls at
checkpoints. American troops seeking to flush out VC
strongholds had to move warily along jungle trails made
treacherous by mines, booby traps and camouflaged pits
lined with fishhooks. Ho continued to send men, materials,
food and munitions to the Viet Cong, despite over a year of
daily bombing of the North, over railroads, highways, and
bridges that had been persistently hit, persistently rebuilt.

French journalist Michèle Ray, who was captured by the
Viet Cong and traveled with them, reported that she found
the guerrilla fighters and their families "apparently in fine
shape and with an excellent morale, a people living under
incessant bombardments, who can laugh, joke, and go on
living."

In Hanoi the Vietnamese put up uncomplainingly with
the hardships of severe shortages. The rice ration had been
kept up, but there was very little meat or sugar, and no
more than five or six yards of cloth per person a year.
Matches, soap, paper and salt were scarce. Bikes were easy
to obtain and cheap, but spare parts were hard to come
by.

Morale was so high that Ho had no hesitation in letting
foreign journalists send out dispatches without censorship.
He also made no attempt, unlike other Communist leaders,
to jam broadcasts of the *Voice of America*. Ho felt that
they actually helped him by proving to his people that what
the American government said about the war could not be

trusted. After being bombed on December 13 and 14, for example, the people of Hanoi heard the *Voice of America* broadcast a denial that there had been any raids on their city.

A commission sent by British philosopher Bertrand Russell, who deplored the war, arrived in North Vietnam to study possible war crimes in the American bombings of nonmilitary targets in Hanoi, including hospitals, schools, homes and open streets. The commission found a great deal of evidence of civilian devastation, but was inclined to believe, as Ho did, that it was accidental. Nevertheless, when the air raid siren wailed, few people lost any time in getting into the ashcan-sized concrete shelters in Hanoi's streets.

The Russians and Chinese were both eager to send experts to join General Giap and advise him in war strategy. Ho tactfully but firmly declined their offers. Russian experts were only allowed to train the first Vietnamese crews in operation of the SAM missile sites. After that they were thanked and sent home. Ho was determined that Hanoi would run its own war and make its own decisions.

In that way, too, neither Moscow nor Peking could complain that one was favored over the other. Even when Moscow sought to confer the Order of Lenin on Ho for his "contributions to the struggle against imperialism," Ho politely asked the Russians to postpone the award "until our people have driven off the United States imperialist aggressors and completely liberated our fatherland."

The Russians had trained some young North Vietnamese pilots to fly MIG-21 fighter planes in the Soviet Union, and at the end of 1966 sent them home with the planes. Observers from Communist Eastern Europe were astonished to see the pilots get up at 4:00 A.M., like most of the population, work in the cold water of the rice paddies for four hours, then get in their planes to fly against American bombers coming in to attack Hanoi.

When a bomber was shot down by a MIG or missile and its pilot bailed out, he was often taken into custody by peasants armed with pitchforks or rifles, and marched off to prison, sometimes none too gently. Diplomats in Hanoi reported that American prisoners were fairly well treated, but suffered from the Vietnamese rice diet.

In February 1967 the *New York Times* military expert estimated that the United States had lost 1,750 planes in the Southeast Asia theater. The Defense Department announced that over sixty-six hundred American troops had been killed and over thirty-seven thousand wounded. By March the U.S. military forces in Vietnam had been built up to a total of four hundred twenty-seven thousand.

Ho, now seventy-seven and beginning to weary, relinquished some of his decision-making powers to his subordinates. He knew that he could not live much longer, and sought to prepare a gradual transfer of power to trusted followers so that his country's struggle could continue smoothly without him.

In his "favorite nephew," Premier Pham Van Dong, whom Ho still called "my other self," he knew he would have a faithful echo of his spirit from beyond the grave, and a spokesman who would follow his policy of balancing off Peking with Moscow. Dong's determination, too, matched his own. "We shall win, we shall win!" Dong insisted. "We shall fight as long as there is one American on our soil!"

He, too, was prepared for another twenty years of war,

and was confident that the new generation of North Vietnamese, who had grown up at war, would fight even more fiercely.

Le Duan, head of the Lao Dong party, was partly of Chinese extraction. "He talks, thinks and acts like a Chinese," Khrushchev once complained. But Le Duan, who had spent ten years in a French prison, followed Ho's example and usually sought to remain neutral between Moscow and Peking. He was more impatient than Ho with the guerrilla war of the Viet Cong in the south, however, urging the commitment of a large North Vietnamese army to drive out the Americans.

In this dissent Le Duan was opposed by Truong Chinh, the leading theoretician of Ho's government. A loyal adherent of Mao Tse-tung, Chinh annoyed the other Hanoi leaders by his open advocacy of Chinese-style Communism. He favored continuation of guerrilla warfare in the south to outlast the Americans and the ARVN, while conserving the north's power for the task of reuniting the country afterward.

The fourth powerful figure in the Ho cabinet was fiery General Vo Nguyen Giap, whose brilliant bicycle-borne war had crushed the French at Dienbienphu in 1954, and who was now deputy premier as well as defense minister. Giap told one journalist, "We fought and won against the Mongols in the 13th Century. Now it is the Americans. We are conscious of our historic role. We have shaken the largest country in the world. In the war for independence our people have been fighting for twenty years, one bends or gets stronger." Strongly pro-Russian, with personal animosity toward Chinh, Giap favored a continuation of the struggle by both conventional and guerrilla forces in the south.

He was probably the best-known and most admired Vietnamese after Ho himself. Less well-known were Giap's grim views about the expendability of human life. "Every minute 100,000 men die all over the world," he once declared. "The life and death of human beings means nothing."

These, then, were the men into whose hands Ho prepared to pass his power as his time on earth grew shorter.

Meanwhile he noted with satisfaction that the Johnson administration was in increasing difficulties. Its officials and generals had kept proclaiming that victory was in sight, and victory did not come. The president had told the American people that they could afford both guns and butter—but with the military budget up to $80 billion, prices were soaring and taxes climbing.

CBS correspondent Eric Sevareid declared on January 24, 1967, that in twenty-five years of Washington reporting, he had never seen as much disbelief in the assertions of any administration as that provoked by Lyndon Johnson's "credibility gap."

Even the Senate's staunchest hawk, John Stennis, said gloomily, "Under existing circumstances, the American people must be prepared for a long-drawn-out and bloody war of attrition in Vietnam . . . which may result in our being tied down in those steaming jungles for ten years or more. . . . It is sad but true that many of the 6-year-old youngsters who started to school this year can expect some time in their lives to patrol the swamps and mountains of Vietnam."

In contrast, the morale of Ho's own people and troops had never been higher. An Atlanta infantry major named Beckwith admitted to U.S. reporters that the VC and North Vietnamese were "the finest soldiers I have ever seen in the world except Americans." He added ruefully, "I wish we could recruit them. I wish we knew what they were drugging them with to make them fight like that. They are highly motivated and highly dedicated."

The American forces still felt compelled to do all the fighting themselves. They had nothing but contempt for the ARVN who spent far more time looting in the villages than they did even in pretended combat.

On February 10, 1967, Ho received a direct message from President Johnson, who urged him to agree to peace talks.

"If we fail to find a just and peaceful solution," the president declared, "history will judge us harshly." He was making this direct appeal, he added, to be certain that no intermediary between them could distort his proposal.

"I am prepared to order a cessation of bombing against your country and the stopping of further augmentation of United States forces in South Vietnam as soon as I am assured that infiltration into South Vietnam . . . has stopped," the president offered. And he proposed a cease-fire to be followed by secret peace talks in Burma or elsewhere.

Five days later the answer came from Ho:

> The Vietnamese people have never done any harm to the United States. But contrary to the pledges made by its representative at the 1954 Geneva Conference, the U.S. Government has ceaselessly intervened in Viet-

nam; it has unleashed and intensified the war of aggression in South Vietnam with a view to prolonging a partition of Vietnam and turning South Vietnam into a neocolony and a military base of the United States. For over two years now, the U.S. Government has with its air and naval forces carried the war to [our] independent and sovereign country.

The U.S. Government has committed war crimes. . . . In South Vietnam, half a million U.S. and satellite troops have resorted to the most inhuman weapons and the most barbarous methods of warfare, such as napalm, toxic chemicals and gases, to massacre our compatriots, destroy crops and raze villages to the ground. In North Vietnam, thousands of U.S. aircraft have dropped hundreds of thousands of tons of bombs, destroying towns, villages, factories, roads, bridges, dikes, dams and even churches, pagodas, hospitals, schools.

In your message, you apparently deplored the sufferings and destruction in Vietnam. May I ask you: Who has perpetrated these monstrous crimes? . . . Our just cause enjoys strong sympathy and support from the peoples of the whole world, including broad sections of the American people.

The U.S. Government has unleashed the war of aggression in Vietnam. It must cease this aggression. That is the only way to the restoration of peace. . . . If the U.S. Government really wants these talks, it must first of all stop unconditionally its bombing raids and all other acts of war. . . . The Vietnamese people will never submit to force, they will never accept talks under the threat of bombs.

14

Dissent Sweeps America

JOHNSON ORDERED General Westmoreland to intensify the military pressure on Ho. On March 27, 1967, the AP noted, "The United States has devised a new method of fighting which consists in penetrating the Vietcong area, concentrating the population into resettlement camps, then burning and destroying everything that remains."

A U.S. General Accounting Office study later revealed that over half the five hundred thousand "refugees from Communism" had received no help of any kind, despite millions of U.S. dollars given to the Saigon regime for their relief. Many of the evacuees had died of disease, thirst or starvation.

If many claims of the American military were suspect, some made by the Viet Cong for propaganda purposes verged on the absurd. One guerrilla newspaper carried the story of four girl partisans who had stopped an advance by two thousand American troops. When journalist Michèle Ray pointed out to the VC that this was wholly implausible, she was told, "We must have dreams. Do you know why the 'puppets' fight so poorly? They have no dreams."

The desertion rate of the ARVN, which was now the third largest army in Asia, climbed to ten thousand a month in the spring of 1967. Most ARVN deserters took their American weapons with them to sell to the Viet Cong on the black market. The ARVN soldier, reported Mike Wallace of CBS-TV, was no patriot: "He feels no kinship, no sense of involvement in the concerns of the Saigon Government." Wallace noted that, in contrast, the VC and North Vietnamese were superb fighters, disciplined both in battle and in village behavior:

"They are more strongly motivated; they feel a deeper sense of kinship with their top leaders, a deeper involvement in the cause for which they fight."

The ARVN forces continued to alienate the people of South Vietnam by massacring women and children, sometimes throwing bodies into trenches and blowing them up with mines to prevent identification. Villages were bombed on the mere suspicion that they were harboring VC. One U.S. pilot of an observation plane called for such an air strike when he spotted a peasant running into a grove of trees. Reporter Jonathan Schell asked the pilot how he could be sure the peasant was a VC.

"Well," the pilot explained, "he walked real proud, with a kind of bounce in his gait, like a soldier, instead of just shuffling along, like the farmers do."

Ho followed with keen interest reports of huge anti-war demonstrations in New York and San Francisco. The World Council of Churches was now demanding direct negotiations with the Viet Cong. In May Dr. Martin Luther

King declared, "Every young man in this country who believes that this war is abominable and unjust should file as a conscientious objector." He compared the testing of new weapons in Vietnam to the Nazis' experiments on concentration camp victims.

Johnson, alarmed at the surging tide of dissent, brought General Westmoreland home to address Congress and express dismay over "recent unpatriotic acts here at home." Senate doves indignantly criticized the president for using Westmoreland to try to stifle dissent by making criticism of Johnson's Vietnam policy seem an act of treason.

"The debate will go on and it will have its price," the president replied on May 2. "It is a price our democracy must be prepared to pay, and the angriest voices of dissent should be prepared to acknowledge." He criticized Dr. King, along with the noted baby specialist, Dr. Spock, for urging that draft-age youth should refuse to serve in Vietnam.

Vice President Humphrey, with a group of congressional doves, drafted and signed a warning to Ho Chi Minh not to misinterpret the great debate in America over the war as meaning that Congress would force a unilateral withdrawal of U.S. troops from South Vietnam. When Humphrey rose to speak at a National Book Award ceremony, novelist Mitchell Goodman shouted, "Mr. Vice President, we are burning children in Vietnam and you and we are all responsible!"

Then fifty noted writers and editors walked out.

Support for Ho's cause was vehement in radical groups like the Students for a Democratic Society (SDS) and the New Left. Former SDS vice president Paul Booth declared,

"Under Ho I'm sure land would be redistributed, and the government and the aristocracy would be out of power. Also, there's no question that Vietnam would be independent. After all, Ho has kept China from running North Vietnam; there's no reason why he couldn't keep them out of South Vietnam."

By summer the American argument over Vietnam had become harsh and bitter, polarizing the nation. The majority of Americans supported the president, taking the traditional view, "My country, right or wrong." They considered dissent disloyal because it "let down the boys fighting for us."

The dissenters insisted that sending American boys to fight in Vietnam had been an unjust and wrong decision, as well as a violation of the president's own promise. The best way to save the troops there from being killed and maimed, they argued, was to bring them home quickly from a war that was unpopular, unable to be won, and condemned by the world.

There were violent clashes between radical dissenters, who burned draft cards and American flags, and right-wing superpatriots who attacked anti-war demonstrations.

Newsweek editor Emmet John Hughes, returning from a trip around the world, reported that in every capital he had visited, not a single minister or diplomat privately supported the American position in Vietnam, whatever they might say in public. All had voiced regret over the American escalation, and hoped for U.S. withdrawal as soon as possible.

Undeterred, Johnson increased the number of American troops in South Vietnam to five hundred twenty-five thousand by June. After visiting Saigon, MacNamara reported that still more men would be needed, but assured Americans that victory was now in sight.

"These generalizations of progress would be more reassuring," said Senator Mansfield, "if they had not been heard from American leaders in Vietnam at many other times." He urged the administration to turn the whole problem over to the United Nations. Meanwhile the Joint Economic Committee revealed that the war would cost the American people $26 billion for 1967 alone, in addition to the $44 billion spent by the Defense Department.

Ho laughed when he read journalist Bernard Fall's report of the despair of an American official in Saigon who was expected to whip up hatred for Ho in South Vietnam.

"You know," the official sighed, "it's damned difficult to tell people to hate a guy who looks like a half-starved Santa Claus . . . and that a frail 77-year-old gentleman with a wispy beard and rubber sandals, ruling a country the size of Florida with an army about as big as the Swiss militia and a 100-plane air force, is a threat to the freedom of Southeast Asia and to America's position in the world."

Ho realized that for the United States Vietnam was only a "side issue" in the struggle against the Soviet Union and Red China for world predominance.

Ho agreed with the views of the noted economist Eliot Janeway, who considered the Soviet Union happy to have the United States bogged down in a land war in Southeast Asia, where Washington was wasting its treasure, manpower, and prestige, while the cost of Moscow's support of Ho was trifling by comparison. The Russians were also

happy to have Washington menace Red China for them, so
that Peking was not free to mobilize large forces against the
USSR.

Senate doves pointed out that despite the SEATO agreements, Britain, France, and Pakistan had refused to send
troops to join the Americans in Vietnam. The only Southeast Asian countries which had sent token forces depended
upon American aid, trade and protection, and many had
sold their troops to Washington for an undisclosed price.
The NATO powers were not only opposed to the war, but
considered it folly because American interests were not
really involved.

Huge demonstrations in England, France, Scandinavia,
and West Germany expressed support for American anti-
war protesters. The one-sided Bertrand Russell international tribunal, sitting in judgment on the United States,
pronounced it guilty of the crimes of aggression and
genocide. French President Charles de Gaulle called the
American intervention in Vietnam "an unjust . . . hateful
war since it brings about the destruction of a small country
by a big one."

English critics pointed out that the Chinese were no-
where in Southeast Asia, but that over half a million American troops were operating not only in Vietnam, but also
secretly in Cambodia, Thailand, and Laos.

In America, disgusted Republicans pointed out that it
was costing the American government three hundred thou-
sand dollars to kill each enemy soldier, in support of a
Saigon dictatorship that suppressed all political opposition.
How, they demanded, did this fantastic expenditure serve
America's interests?

When the flamboyant Premier Ky paid a state visit to Australia, he was denounced by the leader of the opposition Labour Party as "a murderer, a little miserable butcher, a gangster Quisling." That may have been the last straw, because Ky was suddenly downgraded to vice president, and General Nguyen Van Thieu became chief of state.

The "real elections" Ky had been forced to promise were held in September. Ten non-Communist opponents of the Thieu-Ky regime charged that all political rivals had been jailed, exiled or forbidden to run. General Loan's national police terrorized the polling places and counted the ballots themselves. Citizens were threatened with arrest for failing to vote. Thieu was forced to admit that many soldiers had been instructed to vote twice.

President Johnson called the elections a "heartening expression of democracy in Southeast Asia." But even the U.S. Embassy in Saigon conceded that they had been rigged. Senator Robert Kennedy called them "a fraud and a farce," and joined Senators Jacob Javits, Stuart Symington, John Pastore, and a dozen others in demanding that Washington insist on genuine elections in South Vietnam.

"The country is deeply troubled and highly dubious about this war," Javits declared when the polls showed that only 37 percent of the American people approved of the president's handling of the war. In October 1967 a massive two-day peace demonstration was staged in Washington.

From Saigon, Ambassador Ellsworth Bunker and General Westmoreland hastened to assure the American people that the war was going splendidly, with "light at the end of the tunnel" clearly visible. On January 17, 1968, the president declared, "The enemy has been defeated in battle after battle. . . . The number of South Vietnamese living in areas under government protection tonight has grown by more than a million since January of last year." He also hinted that Hanoi would soon have to be forced to agree to negotiations.

Ho and Giap, meanwhile, were carefully preparing a devastating blow aimed at proving to Americans that they were being deceived about the progress of the war, and about the amount of territory U.S. forces and the ARVN controlled. To offset the American advantage of air and sea power, Giap sought to catch Westmoreland off guard.

The NLF proclaimed a cease-fire for the Lunar New Year (Tet) celebrations. Half the ARVN troops defending the cities in South Vietnam went home for the holidays to enjoy the feasts, fireworks, streets covered in flowers and women dressed in festival finery. Then, on the night of January 29, Giap gave the signal. Over two hundred thousand VC and North Vietnamese troops launched a full-scale attack against 37 city and province capitals throughout South Vietnam.

"Compatriots," urged the VC radio network, "the revolution we waited and yearned for has broken out. Everybody must stand up and launch attacks against the Thieu-Ky clique!"

The offensive was a stunning blow to the American military, destroying their claim to have the Viet Cong reeling in defeat. The "pacification" program was also exposed as a paper accomplishment, with almost the entire countryside now completely under the control of the Viet Cong.

But the cost of Ho's psychological victory was a terrible one. In one month of bitter fighting, a fifth of the guerrilla army—over forty-two thousand three hundred troops—was wiped out, largely by massive air attacks. Of all the capitals attacked, only Hué fell, and was held for less than a month.

The American military quickly branded the Tet offensive a failure that had seriously weakened Communist military strength in the south. But the shocked American public, angry at having believed continual military assurances that the enemy had been virtually annihilated before Tet, lost all faith in the administration's war policies. A Gallup Poll survey found 49 percent of the American people now convinced that U.S. intervention in Vietnam had been a blunder.

On March 9 Westmoreland urged the president to send him an additional two hundred six thousand troops in addition to the four hundred seventy-five thousand U.S. forces already there. But Ho's psychological victory was now compelling Johnson to reconsider his goal of a military solution in Vietnam. Rejecting Westmoreland's request, he announced that fewer than fifty thousand would be sent.

Both ARVN and American troops responded to the Tet offensive with unbridled fury. On January 31, NLF political prisoners in Saigon were machine-gunned to death in reprisal. Sergeant James D. Henry, a medic attached to the Thirty-fifth U.S. Infantry, reported that men in his unit herded nineteen Vietnamese women and children together in one village, then machine-gunned them in a heap.

"Such acts are committed out of frustration, fear and hate," Sergeant Henry declared. "Growing disillusionment with our Vietnamese 'allies' and their government . . . gives men less and less reason to get themselves killed. . . . The growing belief that the death of your buddies is for nothing and that it could be your turn next must ultimately lead to a raging hate which requires something to fix on."

The Viet Cong who captured Hué were equally brutal. Almost thirty-five hundred special police, soldiers, government officials, and employees working for the Americans were massacred. Some were mutilated, others buried alive. Almost twelve hundred bodies were thrown into mass graves as the Viet Cong fell back before the marines' siege to retake the city.

Radio Hanoi called the murdered victims, who included women and children, "hooligan lackeys who had incurred blood debts and were therefore annihilated by the Southern armed forces and people." But the atrocities gave the anti-Communist forces justification—and new incentive—for their own acts of terrorism against civilians.

Casualties among American troops, who were often unable to tell friend from foe among peasants in the countryside, mounted heavily during 1968. Many GI's suffered shock as close friends were killed or wounded by invisible snipers, and by hidden mines and booby-traps sometimes set by wives and children of the VC. Some Americans came to see *all* peasants as their enemies, and killed them indiscriminately.

In search-and-destroy missions the Americans not only burned villages, but massacred men, women and children in the same way that brutal ARVN troops had done. At Mylai in March 1968 elements of the Americal Division rounded up women and babies and machine-gunned over a hundred, acting under orders to "destroy Mylai and everything in it." One American captain had told his troops beforehand that they might get a chance "to revenge the deaths of our fellow GI's."

Troops of the Eighty-second Airborne Division raided Song My and executed 502 civilians, 170 of them children. Over one hundred women and children were assembled in one yard and slaughtered with hand grenades and machine gun fire.

News of the terrible massacres at Mylai, Song My and other villages was suppressed by the Americal Division command, and did not leak out until almost two years later. A stunned American people were appalled that U.S. soldiers could have committed such atrocities in the name of fighting a war against Communism.

Disillusionment with the war grew swiftly following the Tet offensive. Senator Fulbright led a fight against the Johnson administration for a greater voice for Congress in limiting and ending the war. Former Ambassador to India John Kenneth Galbraith reminded Americans that a little man in a loincloth, with his people behind him, had driven the powerful British out of India. Only stubborn self-delusion, he warned, could blind Americans to the fact that Ho Chi Minh was the Ghandi of Vietnam.

The universities were now almost all vehemently opposed to the war. "The Vietnam war is the most shameful episode in the whole of American history," declared Harvard's Nobel Prize winner, Professor George Wald, adding, "We are supporting open or thinly disguised military dictatorships all over the world, helping them to control and repress peoples struggling for their freedom."

In bitter Senate debate hawks argued that America had to honor its commitment in Vietnam or lose the respect of the world. Doves pointed out that we would never have the world's respect as long as we continued intervening in Vietnam, whereas France, which had pulled out after a full military defeat, now enjoyed greater prestige than ever.

The Pentagon anxiously flew congressional hawks on junkets to South Vietnam, giving them controlled tours to convince them that the war was being won, and to persuade them to urge the sending of more troops and the spending of more billions in military appropriations. Governor George Romney of Michigan later accused American military and civilian officials in Saigon of "brainwashing" him and other United States visitors.

After Tet, the doves persuaded Senator Eugene McCarthy, a leading opponent of the war, to oppose Johnson for the Democratic presidential nomination. College youngsters from all over America rallied enthusiastically to work for McCarthy in the New Hampshire primary elections on March 12. McCarthy scored a stunning upset by winning in one of the most pro-war states of the Union. Three days later Senator Robert Kennedy suddenly announced that he, too, would oppose the president for renomination, also as a peace candidate.

These unexpected challenges from within his own party to a president who wanted a second term were almost unprecedented in American history. They reflected polls showing Johnson's popularity at an all-time low. The president made a difficult decision and announced it to the American people on a TV broadcast, March 31, 1968.

He would not run for re-election, he revealed. He also declared that he had decided to halt the bombing raids over the upper three-quarters of North Vietnam. Both moves, he said, were intended as proofs of his sincerity in wanting to end the war. He urged Ho to begin peace talks.

In Hanoi, Ho was deluged with congratulations. Clearly he had been right in urging patience and perseverance. The Americans were becoming tired of the war and disillusioned with it. And the Tet offensive had been a master stroke.

Now, at last, Ho agreed to peace talks.

End of a Legend

AFTER CONSIDERABLE DICKERING, Paris was agreed upon by both sides as the site of the peace conference. W. Averell Harriman, former U.S. ambassador to Russia, headed the American delegation. Thieu sent Ky to represent Saigon. Ho's delegate was Xuan Thuy, a veteran Hanoi diplomat. The NLF sent Mrs. Nguyen Thi Binh, once imprisoned by the French. Ky kept raising objections to her presence at the talks. Mrs. Binh called the Thieu regime "a bunch of traitors."

In Washington Senator McGovern denounced Ky as a "little tinhorn dictator" who was stalling the conference to keep the war going. He urged Washington to light a fire under Thieu and Ky by beginning to withdraw troops from Vietnam.

The talks bogged down in endless disputes over how the Saigon regime and the NLF, representing the Viet Cong, should be seated at the bargaining table. Harriman was exasperated by Xuan Thuy's refusal to admit that North Vietnam had its own troops fighting beside the VC.

Meanwhile in Hanoi cafes and shops were opening, boats appeared on the park lake and the women blossomed out in new spring clothes. The newspaper *Hanoi Moi* complained that workers were no longer surpassing industry quotas, and absenteeism was increasing. Worried, Dong told Ho that their war effort was slackening because the bombing of the heavily populated upper north had stopped, and the people were optimistic now that peace talks were finally taking place.

Ho wryly pointed out to Dong how ironic it was that the Americans, who had thought they were demoralizing the North Vietnamese by their bombing raids, had actually only united the country in determined sacrifice. But now that the Americans had stopped bombing for the most part, discouraged, the fighting spirit of Ho's people had been softened!

The war continued to grind on, meanwhile, with the VC making intensive mortar and rocket attacks on Saigon, Hué, and other cities. Thieu accused Ho of ordering the shelling to influence the imminent Democratic National Convention in Chicago to reject the presidential candidacy of Vice President Hubert Humphrey, who supported the Johnson policy in Vietnam, and choose a Senate dove instead.

Giap was, indeed, proving that Hanoi's forces, not the ARVN or U.S. troops, controlled the countryside. But if Ho had his eye on Chicago, he was also signalling Harriman in Paris that there could be no peace settlement without a new coalition government in Saigon that included the NLF.

Ho was surprised and upset when, after all the uproar over the war in America, the political conventions ended by giving the American people a choice of three candidates, not one of whom sought a swift end to the war. Humphrey, for the Democrats, was pledged to continue Johnson's war policy. Richard Nixon, the Republican choice, had been one of the first hawks to advocate intervention and was now deliberately vague about Vietnam. George Wallace, a third party candidate, urged an even greater escalation of the war.

In September, with the Paris talks still bogged down in preliminaries, Truong Chinh warned the North Vietnamese on Radio Hanoi not to expect an early end to the fighting.

On October 31 President Johnson suddenly announced a cessation of all bombing north of the Seventeenth Parallel. He declared that a secret understanding had been reached at Paris by which Communist attacks on South Vietnam's cities would stop, both sides would respect the demilitarized zone between the two Vietnams, and both the Saigon regime and the NLF would be represented in the peace talks.

Thieu, stunned, angrily announced that his government would bargain only with Hanoi, not the Viet Cong. Washington sharply called him into line, and Thieu backed down.

When Nixon replaced Johnson in the White House, he sent Henry Cabot Lodge as his chief negotiator in the Paris peace talks. On January 18, 1969, expanded negotiations finally began. But month after month no progress was made in reaching a political settlement of the war that was now the costliest, most unsuccessful, and most unpopular in American history. By February 22 over five hundred forty-two thousand, five hundred U.S. troops were tied down in South Vietnam, and Hanoi claimed to have shot over thirty-two hundred American planes out of the skies.

On the eighth anniversary of the founding of the Viet Cong, Lin Piao sent Red China's greetings: "Under the leadership of their great president, Ho Chi Minh, and persevering in a protracted people's war, the 31 million Vietnamese people will surely drive out all the U.S. aggressors from Vietnam, and achieve the great goals of liberating the South, defending the North and re-unifying their fatherland. . . . Their struggle is our struggle. The 700 million Chinese people provide powerful support for the Vietnamese people."

Ho knew that Peking was keeping a careful eye on secret American military bases in Laos and Thailand. As long as the Chinese felt threatened by Washington's ring of military bases around them, Mao would continue to give Ho everything he needed to keep the Americans bogged down in Vietnam.

When the Paris talks indicated that Washington was trying to force terms on Hanoi at the peace table that it had not been able to win on the battlefield, Ho firmly announced in May, "Peace will come only when all American aggressor troops are completely swept out of our country, and the puppet traitors are overthrown. I look forward to hearing of great and glorious new victories!"

The new Nixon administration considered Ho's tough talk simply rhetoric intended to strengthen Xuan Thuy's bargaining position in Paris. But Ho instructed Thuy to remind the Americans that when the Vietnamese had defeated the Ming Chinese invaders in the fifteenth century, they had graciously provided their enemies with horses and supplies to get them swiftly back home. "Tell the Americans," Ho said ironically, "we will be very happy to do the same for them."

President Nixon countered with a plan to end America's involvement in ground fighting by "Vietnamizing" the war, reversing what Westmoreland had done in having Americans take over infantry combat from the ARVN. Nixon ordered U.S. units in Vietnam to train and arm the ARVN to replace them, promising a gradual withdrawal of U.S. units as the ARVN were able to fight more and more of Saigon's war.

Ho saw this plan as an attempt by the president to save face by pretending the war had not been lost. Ho had no doubts about dealing swiftly and easily with the ARVN, once the American forces had left. But he was surprised that, after Johnson's downfall because of the war, the American people were apparently willing to give Nixon up to four years, perhaps longer, to get U.S. troops out of Vietnam.

Already casualties had reached thirty-nine thousand dead, two hundred fifty-five thousand wounded. And since 1961 over half a million North Vietnamese alone had been killed, mostly by American bombing.

Now seventy-nine, Ho knew that his frail body would not last much longer. In August he decided to write a letter to Nixon appealing for a settlement of the war through mutual concessions. The president failed to respond, and did not communicate Ho's appeal to Lodge in Paris. Nixon persisted with his Vietnamization policy. Each time new peace demonstrations threatened to erupt, he would hastily announce a token withdrawal of a few troops with promises of bigger withdrawals to come.

"Peace was possible in 1968," AP correspondent Peter Harnett declared. "The Johnson Administration had decided that a military victory was not possible. The South Vietnamese didn't like it, but they were prepared for a political settlement. I remember driving through the delta and the Americans and the Vietnamese were deciding which hamlets would fly the Viet Cong flag and which the South Vietnamese flag when the great day of ceasefire finally came. But Mr. Nixon let the moment for peace go by. For the Vietnamese people, that was a tragedy."

Ho did not live to see peace restored to his country, nor his dream of a united, independent Vietnam realized.

On September 3, 1969, a monsoon downpour drenched Hanoi. During the dreary morning, loudspeakers throughout the city suddenly came alive with a mournful bulletin: "Comrade Ho Chi Minh, Chairman of the Central Committee of the Workers' Party and President of the Democratic Republic of Vietnam, died at 0947 hours after a grave and sudden heart attack."

The North Vietnamese were stunned. It seemed incredible that Uncle Ho, who had guided their lives and led their struggles for forty years, had finally left them. For a whole week all the country's newspapers ran black-bordered portraits of the leader who had been revered as the greatest Vietnamese in their two-thousand-year history.

Ho's body lay in state, in front of a huge portrait of him flanked by burning incense, in the Congress Hall of Ba Dinh Square, where twenty-four years earlier he had first proclaimed his country's independence. Tens of thousands of peasants, soldiers, and government officials, all wearing mourning bands, filed slowly past his bier for a last view of the little leader who, in death, still wore his peasant tunic.

The NLF announced that it would observe a seventy-two-hour cease-fire in Ho's honor. American generals were baffled. "We can hardly agree to a ceasefire honoring a man who has been our No. 1 enemy since this war started," one declared. But a private agreement for a cease-fire was arranged with no public acknowledgment of it by the Americans.

Thieu was furious. "Why should I observe the Communists' ceasefire?" he fumed. "Would Hanoi lay down its guns for 72 hours if *I* died?" Although he was pressured to go along with the truce, he reneged and gave orders for ARVN troops to attack the VC. Outraged, General Abrams tried to contact Thieu, but was told he had "gone fishing." The angered VC counterattacked heavily, and called upon South Vietnamese to honor Ho's memory by expressing sorrow in revolutionary acts.

President Nixon refused to comment on Ho's death, but one Washington official was quoted by *Newsweek* as saying, "The atmosphere in the White House since Ho left the scene is something close to elation."

The most interesting reactions came from Saigon, capital of the war effort against Ho. An editorial in the Saigon *Vietnamese Guardian* paid the dead leader a grudging tribute:

> With his passing, for better and for worse, Vietnam loses its unique politician of truly international status. With President Ho's death, a legendary, almost mytho-

logical figure disappears from the international political scene.

One Saigon journalist admitted, "Our problem has been that we didn't have a national hero. Now that Ho Chi Minh is dead, North and South are on the same basis."

Even those who had left the north for Saigon in the emigration of 1954 were sorrowful. *Commonweal*, the liberal Catholic weekly, reported the typical comment of one old woman street vendor in Saigon: "He was an old and gentle person. All who know him agree. Even in his important position he stayed close to the people. . . . He never married and so he lived for the country, Vietnam. We were all his relatives."

A Saigon pedicab driver who had left Hanoi as a strong anti-Communist told an American reporter, "Ho was the only true leader of our country in the last 20 or 30 years. He may or may not have been a real Communist, but every Vietnamese knows he was a real nationalist. He lived only for the Vietnamese nation. I am a poor man and our country is a poor country. Uncle Ho was always very close to the poor people. Not like the people in the Saigon government, who hide behind the police guns and live in big houses. I am a Catholic. But if you, Mr. American, do not understand that we love Uncle Ho, you do not understand our people."

The American military wondered whether Ho's death would cause serious morale problems for the Viet Cong. There was also speculation that discord might now break out between the pro-Soviet and pro-Chinese leaders of Hanoi, with Ho no longer there to restrain and balance them.

Worried about the same thing, and each seeking its own advantage, Moscow and Peking rushed envoys to Ho's funeral. Chinese Premier Chou En-lai flew into Hanoi first and went into lengthy conferences with the cabinet. Next day, leaving aides behind, he flew back to Peking to avoid an embarrassing meeting with incoming Soviet Premier Aleksei Kosygin, who also conferred with the cabinet.

Both Communist premiers were assured that Ho had carefully arranged for a tranquil succession of power to his deputies, who would continue to rule in collective leadership. Since Le Duan was honored by being selected to make Ho's funeral oration, it was assumed that as secretary of the Lao Dong party, he would be "first among equals."

The other equals were Premier Pham Van Dong and National Assembly Leader Truong Chinh, with Defense Minister Vo Nguyen Giap a notch lower in the hierarchy. But it quickly became clear that all were committed to be the faithful executors of Ho Chi Minh's political testament, and had no intention of falling out among themselves or of abandoning their dead leader's policies or dreams.

The funeral rites were simple, in accordance with Ho's wishes that "great funerals should be avoided in order not to waste the time and money of the people." But one hundred thousand Vietnamese wearing white mourning dress jammed Ba Dinh Square, while another million listened to the ceremony over loudspeakers around Hanoi. Le Duan read a brief oration in a voice quivering with emotion.

Promising that Ho "will always be there to guide us," Le Duan read the dead leader's own last message to them, conveying the "boundless affection" Uncle Ho had always felt for all his "nephews and nieces."

Ho expressed his grief that the Communist world was riven and divided. But he promised, "We are sure to win total victory. . . . Our rivers, our mountains, our men will always remain. When the Americans are defeated, we will build our country ten times more beautiful." The usually expressionless Vietnamese yielded to outbursts of weeping and cries of grief.

On October 15 and again in November hundreds of thousands of Americans demonstrated their opposition to continuing the war under Nixon's Vietnamization plan. Two weeks later the president announced that he planned to withdraw all U.S. ground combat forces on a secret time-table, and asked for the support of the "great silent major-ity" of Americans.

Polarization over the war grew even more intense and angry during 1970. The country was thrown into further uproar in May when Nixon sent American troops into Cambodia to attack North Vietnamese and VC sanctuaries along Vietnam's western border. The president defended his decision as essential to protect American troops during his program of gradual withdrawal. As justification, he pointed to large caches of Communist military supplies which had been captured. Anti-war critics accused him of widening the war into an Indo-Chinese conflict, with fight-ing now flaring up all over Cambodia.

Doves in the Senate began an unsuccessful fight to pass legislation which would force the president to end the unde-clared war still raging almost ten years after the first Amer-ican soldier had been killed in combat on the soil of Vietnam, seven thousand miles away. But two years after

Nixon's election, there were still almost four hundred thousand American troops in the war zone.

"I suppose the war has come to the same stage where we thought we were in 1963," admitted General Paul D. Harkins, who had headed the first American military command in South Vietnam under President Kennedy. "They're still talking about how many killed this week and how much of the population is under control. . . . We went in there in 1954 to help the Vietnamese. Then the Laotians in 1959. Then the Thais in 1962. And now we're helping the last country there—Cambodia. We've helped everybody. . . . It's confusing."

Communist or not, Ho Chi Minh will probably go down in history as a great Vietnamese patriot who was one of the extraordinary world figures of this century. Selfless, courageous, dedicated to Vietnamese independence at all costs, he wrestled France to her knees and fought the United States, the world's mightiest power, to a military stalemate.

His single-minded resolution changed the course of history, polarized public opinion in the United States, forced an American president to withdraw from seeking a second term, and radicalized millions of admiring youth around the world who demonstrated in his support chanting, "Ho, Ho, Ho Chi Minh!"

Ho's unique mixture of Marxism, paternalism, and intense nationalism was enormously successful in inspiring tremendous sacrifice among his people. They also loved "Bac Ho" (Uncle Ho) for his winning personal modesty and gentle ways. Ho was the despair of all his enemies—the

French, the Saigon regime, the Americans—because they were unable to muster hatred of him. He was held in as much affection in South Vietnam as among the people he led in the north.

Not the least of his great achievements was that he had, like Tito, achieved a "national Communism" which kept his country out of the grip of both Red China and the Soviet Union, while he skillfully played one off against the other to get the help his country needed. When he died, North Vietnam was no satellite but a proud, independent country, determined on nationhood for all Vietnamese.

Against Ho it could be said that he had been ruthless in his betrayal to the French of political rivals or non-Communist cadres in the independence movement, to be rid of them. His dream of a united, free Vietnam had cost his people a dreadful price in devastation and bloodshed. He also had to be held responsible for the savage counter-terror which the Viet Cong inflicted upon southern city and village officials of the Saigon regime and their families, as well as for Truong Chinh's excesses during the ill-conceived land reform program following the Geneva Accords.

But when the books of his life are balanced, and peace is finally restored to the tragic land of Vietnam, Ho Chi Minh will always be known to the peasants who loved and followed him as the greatest Vietnamese in their history—the revered uncle of his country.

Bibliography and
Suggested Further Reading

(*Indicates Recommended Reading)

Archer, Jules. *Battlefield President: Dwight D. Eisenhower.* New York: Julian Messner, 1967.

————. *The Dictators.* New York: Hawthorn Books, Inc., 1967.

*————. *Hawks, Doves and the Eagle.* New York: Hawthorn Books, Inc., 1970.

Buttinger, Joseph. *Vietnam: A Dragon Embattled.* New York: Frederick A. Praeger, 1967.

*Cameron, James. *Here Is Your Enemy.* New York, Chicago, San Francisco: Holt, Rinehart and Winston, 1965.

Committee For Economic Development. *The National Economy and the Vietnam War.* New York: Committee For Economic Development, 1968.

*Corson, William R. *The Betrayal.* New York: W. W. Norton & Company, Inc., 1968.

*Duncan, Donald. *The New Legions.* New York: Random House, 1967.

*Fall, Bernard. *The Two Vietnams.* New York: Frederick A. Praeger, 1963.

*Fishel, Wesley R. and T. A. Bisson. *The United States and Vietnam: Two Views.* New York: Public Affairs Committee, Inc., 1966.

*Galbraith, John Kenneth. *How To Get Out of Vietnam.* New York: The New American Library, 1967.

Gunther, John. *Inside Asia.* New York and London: Harper & Brothers, 1939.

*Halberstam, David. *The Making of a Quagmire.* New York: Random House, 1965.

Janeway, Eliot. *The Economics of Crisis.* New York: Weybright and Talley, 1968.

*Lacouture, Jean. *Ho Chi Minh: A Political Biography.* New York: Random House, 1968.

*Ray, Michèle. *The Two Shores of Hell.* New York: David McKay Company, Inc., 1968.

*Roy, Jules. *The Battle of Dien Bien Phu.* New York: Harper & Row, 1965.

*Salisbury, Harrison E. *Behind the Lines—Hanoi.* New York, Evanston, and London: Harper & Row, 1967.

*Scheer, Robert. *How the United States Got Involved in Vietnam.* Santa Barbara: Center for the Study of Democratic Institutions, 1965.

*Schell, Jonathan. *The Military Half.* New York: Alfred A. Knopf, 1968.

*Senate Republican Policy Committee. *The War In Vietnam.* Washington, D.C.: Public Affairs Press, 1967.

Simone, Vera. *China In Revolution.* Greenwich, Conn. Fawcett Publications, Inc., 1968.

Warburg, James P. *Western Intruders.* New York: Atheneum, 1967.

Wint, Guy. *Spotlight On Asia.* London: Penguin Books, 1959.

Wise, David and Thomas B. Ross. *The Invisible Government.* New York: Random House, 1964.

News items and articles were also consulted in the following periodicals: *Commonweal, Esquire, Foreign Affairs, I. F. Stone's Weekly, Life, Look, Mankind, Monthly Review, Nation, New Republic, Newsweek, New York Times Magazine, New Yorker, Readers' Digest, Reporter, Saturday Evening Post, Scanlon's, Soviet Weekly, University, U.S. News and World Report.*

Index